I Believe In ...

I Believe In ...

Christian,
Jewish, and
Muslim
Young People
Speak About
Their Faith

Pearl Gaskins

Cricket Books
Chicago

Text copyright © 2004 by Pearl Gaskins
All rights reserved
Printed in the United States of America
Designed by Randy A. Martinaitis
Second printing, 2005

Library of Congress Cataloging-in-Publication Data

Gaskins, Pearl Fuyo.
    I believe in— : Christian, Jewish, and Muslim young people speak about their faith / Pearl Gaskins.
        p. cm.
    Includes bibliographical references.
    ISBN 0-8126-2713-X
    1. Faith. 2. Teenagers—Religious life. I. Title.
BL626.3.G37 2004
200'.835—dc22   2004001146

Dedication

In remembrance of my friend Alice. Some of my first conversations about religion and the afterlife occurred in the cul-de-sac in front of her house when we were teenagers. We disagreed about everything but remained friends anyway.

Contents

Acknowledgments

When Marc Aronson, former publisher of Cricket Books, suggested that I create this book, I was dubious. My first book, *What Are You? Voices of Mixed-Race Young People* (Henry Holt, 1999), which Marc edited, was about the mixed-race experience, something I had lived and knew personally and intimately. But I knew little about religion, and there was so much to know. Despite my shortcomings and the breadth and complexity of the subject matter this book was born. Marc's vision and his confidence in me made this possible.

This book is a collaboration between myself and the generous young people who tell their stories in these pages. They sat down with me in their living rooms, houses of worship, school cafeterias, and workplaces, and they educated me. They recounted and reflected upon the evolution of their faiths. They admitted to confusion, doubt, and temptation. And most of all, they had the courage to commit to print a part of themselves that is still evolving.

Many people assisted me in my research. First there are the experts who are quoted in the book.

Then there are the many people and organizations that steered me to articulate interviewees and talented young writers, or suggested resources on religion. They include: Eboo Patel, Interfaith Youth Core; Safa Zarzour, Universal School; David M. Rosenberg, Newberger Hillel Center, University of Chicago; Muslim Student Association of the University of Illinois at Chicago; Dirk Ficca and Josh Borkin, Council for a Parliament of the World's Religions; Pat Pacer, Catholic Youth Office, Archdiocese of Chicago; Patty Jane Pelton, St. Francis Xavier Parish; Jorge Rivera, Hispanic Youth Ministry, Archdiocese of Chicago; Islamic Cultural Center of Greater Chicago; Moody Bible Institute; United Synagogue Youth; A TEAM Teen Ministry, Apostolic Church of God; Family School of Chicago; Young Chicago Authors; Nancy Giangrasse, Project A.S.T.R.O. (Art Studies Toward Real Opportunities); Snow City Arts Foundation; Charles Brown, Philosophy Department, William Rainey Harper College; Vietnamese Association of Illinois; Youth for Social Action.

Besides Marc Aronson, others at Cricket Books who nudged me along were Carol Saller and Joëlle Dujardin. They were incredibly patient and supportive.

My husband, Randy Brockway, shares in this and all of my accoplishments. He gives me the space and support to write these books. My life and work have been greatly enriched by his presence.

Introduction

L ast year I received a letter from a seventeen-year-old girl who had just read my first book, *What Are You? Voices of Mixed-Race Young People*, a collection of interviews I conducted with teens and young adults. Karen is mixed race; her biological family, she was told, was Italian, Irish, and North-African Jewish. She was adopted and raised by Jewish-Americans of European origins and identifies as a Jew.

A disturbing story she'd read in my book prompted Karen to write to me. A young woman quoted in my book said officials at the synagogue she had attended for most of her life refused to allow her father to participate in her bat mitzvah because he was not Jewish. A bat mitzvah is a coming-of-age ceremony for Jewish teenage girls. Deeply wounded by the rejection of her interfaith family, the young woman eventually left the synagogue and Judaism.

Saddened by what she had read, Karen wrote that she had never felt excluded or slighted by the Jews of her synagogue because of her background. "My congregation is like an extension of my family," she wrote. "It is perhaps the one place outside of my home that I feel always embraced and accepted." Karen described how her synagogue and her faith had enriched her life. She wrote about studying the Torah in Hebrew and finding poetry and deep meaning in the ancient texts. She recounted singing, laughing, and crying during the annual "Martin Luther King Seder" hosted by her synagogue at Passover to celebrate freedom for all humankind and the dream of a more peaceful world.

Although I am nonreligious, Karen's letter moved me. During my career as a magazine journalist and young-adult author, I have interviewed more than a thousand teens and young adults about every topic imaginable. However, the role of religion in their lives was an area I had left unexplored. For example, when I wrote about dating, I didn't realize that the subject is irrelevant to readers whose religions forbid it. When I spoke with young people in crisis—alcoholics, victims of violence, kids afflicted with AIDS and other life-threatening diseases—I bypassed the part faith played in their recovery. When I interviewed teens about life goals, I didn't ask how religion shaped those aspirations. That was a mistake. So when I was given the opportunity to create a book that explored religion in young people's lives, I was intrigued.

After a little bit of digging, I found that there's a growing body of research on this topic. One of the most respected of the researchers is Christian Smith, professor of sociology at the University of North Carolina at Chapel Hill. Smith is director of the National Study of Youth and Religion, a massive four-year research project using survey data collected from thousands of teenagers around the United States.

"We have reason to believe that religion and spirituality are very significant matters in the lives of many American teenagers," states Smith. More than eighty percent of American teenagers hold some religious affiliation, according to the study. Researchers also found the following to be true about American teens:

- About 35 percent say they attend religious services weekly, and another 15 percent attend at least monthly.
- About 30 percent say that religious faith is extremely important in their lives, and another 30 percent say religious faith is somewhat important in their lives.
- About 40 percent report that they pray daily.
- About 40 percent have participated in a religious youth group for two years or more.
- About 25 percent say that they have been "born again."

These statistics show that a large number of American youth are religious and that many practice their faith. That's not surprising, since religion—its practices, belief systems, and institutions—is a powerful force in our world.

For example, issues involving faith are raised often and loudly. While I worked on this book, my office floor became carpeted with religion-related news stories, many of them prominent front-page articles. They included articles about abortion, cloning, and stem-cell research—controversial issues involving deeply held religious beliefs about the nature and origins of human life.

Other stories described challenges to religious teachings about gender and sexuality. Biblical scholars raised questions about the role of women in the Bible. An openly gay priest was ordained. Gays and lesbians fought religious institutions for the right to marry. Roman Catholic priests were accused of sexual abuse.

The separation of church and state as ordered by the First Amendment was tested. The government's plans to fund religious programs and religious education were debated. A judge was fired after refusing to remove a monument depicting the Ten Commandments from his courthouse lobby. A federal court ruled that the recitation of the Pledge of Allegiance in public schools is unconstitutional because it contains the phrase "under God."

Another stack of stories chronicled religious prejudice and intolerance. A teenager smashed a mosque window as Muslims prayed inside. A Jewish cemetery was desecrated. Thousands of Muslims were deported or detained under the guise of national security. Photos from the Middle East depicted parents grieving over the coffins of dead children.

Although religion was often associated with conflict and controversy, positive stories were no less important. These were dozens of stories about houses of worship that fed needy families, sent aid to war-torn countries, and supported families grieving the loss of loved ones. I was reminded that people of faith are often at the forefront of struggles to create a more just and peaceful world.

Who are religious Americans? They're predominantly Christian. About three out of four adults in the United States identify as Christian, according to the extensive 2001 American Religious Identification Survey.[1] The numbers of Americans who are members of non-Christian religious groups are growing, but they're still very much in the minority. For example, only 1.3 percent of those surveyed identified as Jewish and 0.5 percent reported Muslim. (About 14 percent of survey participants described themselves as nonreligious or secular.)

Depending on where you live, you may or may not know many religious minorities. However, these groups have created thriving communities throughout the United States. The Chicago area where I live and work is home to a growing and diverse Muslim community, including immigrant families from Pakistan, the Middle East, and Bosnia-Herzegovina, and the largest concentration of African-American Muslims in the country. Chicago has a sizeable Jewish-American population—the fifth largest concentration of Jews in the country. There are also communities of Buddhists, Hindus, and Baha'i.

This book is based on interviews with teens and young adults who are

---

[1] This survey was produced by the Graduate Center of the City University of New York.

or were Christians, Jews, and Muslims. I limited the scope of the book to these three important and interconnected faiths. Christianity, Judaism, and Islam trace their origins back to a common patriarch, Abraham, and to a common land, the Middle East. They are monotheistic faiths, or faiths that worship one God—the same God. They share many of the same sacred texts and stories.

When I embarked on this project, my goal was simply to introduce readers to some of the basic beliefs and practices of these faiths and to challenge stereotypical ideas. I think this book accomplishes this and much more. It also illustrates the rich variety of ways that young people approach and understand faith and the incredible diversity among people within the same religion and even the same denomination.

As many of the young people in this book show, thinking about moral, ethical, and religious questions—is there a God? How should I worship? What is a good life?—is part of the religious quest, no matter what answers you choose. I hope that this book will inspire readers in this quest.

How the Book Was Written

This book is a collection of excerpts from interviews I conducted with about ninety-five teens and young adults in the Chicago area between fall 2002 and summer 2003. Most of the interviewees were in their late teens and early twenties. They were current or former Christians, Jews, and Muslims.

I found most of these people by contacting youth programs at Chicago-area churches, synagogues, and mosques. I hung out at malls, college cafeterias, and public events. Interviews were taped, and the tapes were transcribed word for word. Then words and sentences were chipped away, and the narratives emerged. People's words were not changed in editing. However, repetitious phrases and superfluous language—"like," "sort of," "oh," "kind of," "just"— were deleted. When the flow of ideas was confusing, I took the liberty of moving sentences around. Many of the grammatical errors that people commonly make in speech were not corrected.

In almost every case, edited interviews were e-mailed to the interviewee, who was invited to flag errors and quotes taken out of context. Although they were discouraged from doing so, a few people added sentences or a few paragraphs to their narratives. Some participants, or their parents, asked that certain statements be deleted or that a name be changed to disguise an identity. I decided to omit last names after speaking with Muslim-Americans who said their families had received threatening phone calls after the terrorist attacks on the United States on September 11, 2001.

I use the terms "faith" and "religion" interchangeably. The religious descriptions listed beneath people's names are the terms people used to describe themselves. Many people preferred general terms such as Christian, Jew, or Muslim. For example, several Jews disliked what they saw as divisive movement labels of Reform, Conservative, and Orthodox. Many of the Muslims I spoke with embrace a Pan-Muslim identity and resist breakdowns into sects.

Catholics usually referred to themselves as "Catholic" and not "Roman Catholic." Protestants often described themselves as "Christian." Some Protestants called themselves "nondenominational." Leaving self-labeling to interviewees created inconsistencies, but I prefer to use the terms that people are comfortable with rather than to impose a classification system onto them.

In the sections called "My Faith Journey," you'll read longer accounts from people who are not afraid to ask tough faith-shaking questions.

Although some religious terms are defined and basic information about Christianity, Judaism, and Islam is conveyed in the narratives, this book is not a primer on the beliefs and practices of these religions. It conveys the understanding people have of their own faith and others' faiths—not necessarily what religious authorities promulgate. Library and bookstore shelves are filled with books written by experts about Christianity, Judaism, and Islam. I've included a list of books and other resources at the end.

Some of the people quoted in this book criticize or condemn particular religious beliefs and practices, including those of their own faiths. These statements, though controversial and even offensive to some people, are presented so readers can understand how interviewees' faith evolved—what options they gave up and for what reasons. Also, people can be critical of their own faith yet remain engaged with it. That tension, as the book illustrates, often produces spiritual growth and innovative ideas.

I myself have grown from the experience of creating this book, not spiritually, but in other ways. First I was forced to confront my own anxiety about religion. For me, a former Christian, religion has always evoked feelings of being awkward and ignorant—of lip syncing my way through hymns during Sunday services, for example, or not knowing when to stand or sit or kneel. After doing research for this book—in reading about religion, interviewing dozens of people, and visiting houses of worship—I've become less ignorant and less anxious.

This project also forced me to confront my misconceptions about people who are religious. I thought all Evangelical Christians were politically conservative. Then I met a few whose political views are anything but conservative. I talked to Muslim girls who wear the traditional headscarves, yet listen to Eminem and have posters of Ben Affleck on their bedroom walls.

Most of all, I've gained a deep respect for young people who strive to stay true to their religious beliefs. As you'll see, for most of them—Christians, Jews, and Muslims alike—being religious is not an easy road. Some describe their daily struggle to be observant and moral in a temptation-filled world. Others depict a youth culture that labels religion as uncool. Many wrestled with doubts, conflicts, and the prejudices of others. The people I admire most are applying the values their faith taught them to make the world a better place.

You Figure Out What's True to You

When she was younger, Julia was a practicing Jew. Then she was agnostic for a while. Now she's exploring Buddhism and Native American religions. She's uncertain about lots of things, she admits. But she's fearlessly searching for answers.

Julia, 15
No particular religion—still searching

I love pierced lips. I thought: that's cool. I want to do that. And I finally had the chance to. A few months ago, I got it done. My parents weren't really happy about it, but they didn't mind it that much because they probably saw it coming.

Technically, you're not supposed to get piercings, but tons of Jewish girls do. That's why I never had my ears pierced, because my mom was so strict about that. All of these Reform Jewish people don't care about pierced ears. Tattoos, maybe—but piercings they don't see as mutilation. But my mom does, definitely.

My mom is a Reform Jew. My dad, he wasn't really religious when I was younger, but he went along with the whole Jewish thing. He was raised sort of Christian, but not really. He didn't have to go to church every Sunday. But for a long time now he's been getting more into spirituality—he's into Native American stuff, some Tibetan Buddhist stuff. He's Unitarian Universalist, I guess, if he's anything. My parents divorced when I was three or four.

I like Judaism. I went to Sunday school every Sunday until fourth grade, when I just got tired of the snobby kids there. Plus we got this new teacher around that time that barely knew English, and I didn't know much Hebrew. So that lady really confused me, and she was angry all the time. So I stopped going to Sunday school, and I stopped going to temple altogether.

It was nothing against my religion. I was down with God, and Adam and Eve, and all that stuff. I've gotten a lot from Judaism. It's pretty much what my morals still go around—I guess a lot of the world's morals, actually.

MY FAITH JOURNEY

In the Old Testament there are stories of standing up for yourself, not being afraid. In the story of Purim, Esther gets picked to be the new queen for some king. So Esther wants to tell the king about this guy, Haman, who is plotting to kill all the Jews in the village. But the thing is, if she says something, she could get killed. It's kind of like a feminist stand-up-for-yourself thing in the Bible. She says, "I heard that Haman wants to kill all my people. I'm a Jew." The king's like, "Oh, I'll help you." That was great.

I like Cain and Abel. I always think about Adam and Eve. I respect those Bible stories. I try to see deeper. I think the Bible is all metaphorical.

Some of my friends rebel against the Bible. They say, "It's so stupid. Look how much money it's made." Some of them don't care in the first place. They say, "Why should I care about religion? I'm just a kid." They're like, "Science is right, science is proven." But science isn't proven. Science is just another theory. It's really another religion. The Bible is really pretty cool. It has a lot of wise things in it—even if I don't follow it that closely.

Around sixth grade—that's like the bar mitzvah age—my mom started getting worried. She's like, "Julia, I really want you to have a bat mitzvah." I wouldn't go back to Sunday school, but I got a tutor. I learned Hebrew. I learned about the history of Israel and Judaism. I enjoyed it. I liked learning new languages. I was ready to have a bat mitzvah.

But suddenly around the time that I was getting good at Hebrew and stuff, I was exposed to this whole new world of theology. I was in my school library, and I picked up a book about the five major religions, and it was so interesting. And I realized something: how do I know that just because I was raised with this, it's what I really believe? There's so much out there. And suddenly I was like, "Whoa, wait a minute. I can't have a bat mitzvah."

I told my dad, because he would accept that. But when I broke it to my mom, she was a little sad. For a while, she was hoping I would change my mind. But I didn't. So she would be like, "Why are you ashamed of your heritage?" I'm not; I'm proud to be Jewish. It's my heritage. It's not my religion, though. I don't really have a specific religion—it's kind of a mix right now. I definitely believe in some kind of spiritual thing. I don't know what.

Around sixth and seventh grades I went through all of this teenage angst. I was still a little naive about things. Suddenly I looked around and realized, wow, this country is so stupid! I looked at capitalism—OK, it works, but we're being run by corporations. People expect cigarette companies to go away, but they fund our government. I started listening to music that was political. I watched friends do terrible things. I've had friends get really hurt—emotionally, physically, whatever. I was what I'd call agnostic for a while. I started questioning things. It was like: the good Christian God that everyone talks about—he gave us free will. But what kind of God puts people on Earth to serve him and dedicate their lives to him? Is that a good thing?

I noticed around seventh and eighth grades people suddenly were beginning to separate—just slightly. There were the Christian kids, and they'd be like, "No, you're wrong, it's Jesus." In Christianity it's all about spreading the Word and telling everyone what's right. Then there were the kids that were like, "Oh, whatever." They weren't Christian. I didn't know which side to take because I didn't want to lose anybody.

We're Reform, so we weren't hard-core Jewish. We were always open-minded. I never was told that other religions were wrong. I think that whatever you really believe in—that's your truth. And there is no universal truth, which is why I don't yell at people for being a certain religion just because I don't believe in it. Because if they really believe in it, that's what's true in their life.

My dad has always been pretty liberal, and he's opened me up to a lot of things. I grew up with his Native American ideals. One idea I do like—I think it's Lakota Sioux. They believe that there's spirits in everything. There's a River Spirit, Rock Spirit, Eagle Spirit, and then there's the Great Spirit, which is like the Big Guy, Girl, whatever. And he's like God, I guess. I kind of believe that everything is sort of alive. Everything is made up of mass and atoms, so nothing is really dead.

When I was little, I didn't realize that believing in reincarnation wasn't Jewish. I thought, "OK, I'm Jewish, I believe in reincarnation."

I mean I believe in life after life and learning more in each life. That's why some people just don't get it. There's people my age who understand more than fifty-year-olds do. People are at all different stages in their many lives. I think that eventually you reach nirvana—you learned it all and you're enlightened, and you're not so materialistic like everyone around here is.

I guess if anything I'm Buddhist. There's all these different principles I believe in—like Zen. It's the simple, perfect state. It's not perfect, but you understand so much that you don't need to go deeper. It's like the ultimate enlightenment. I don't really know how to explain it because it's kind of like falling in love—you can't explain it until you've had it. And maybe you can't explain it even then.

I think that spirituality is important. It's impossible that we have these amazing minds but this is all there is. How can we exist without something more? One thing that does make me believe that there is a spiritual world is that there's always hope. I always have hope. So I do think it's important— whatever your spirituality may be—that you think about it, that you figure out what's true to you. And I'm still kind of in that process.

I'm closest to Buddhism. But I'm not going to label myself because I don't see reason for having to belong to one specific religion. Everyone customizes religions a little, I think. Even if you're Catholic, I'm sure you have slightly different beliefs than the person next to you.

On My Own

My mom still thinks that I'm ashamed of being Jewish. But I'm not, I'm proud of it. It made me who I am. She just has to see that, and she will. I think she's finally realized that I'm on my own now with religion. She's letting go slowly.

I've been thinking more about my life. Something I've realized is I have the most control over my life. In a way, I'm really my own God. Maybe I am the higher power, and this God that everyone speaks of is really just their conscience in the back of their head.

That kind of scared me. I'm a crazy, chaotic person, and suddenly I'm realizing, wait a minute—I'm the one controlling? I mean, I'm human. I've made some bad decisions. I wish that there was someone else to help me. I mean, even if there is some kind of God, I'm still controlling things. I'm the one that does things.

I always grew up with such freedom, and I think deep inside sometimes I really want control. I wouldn't want to be controlled by my parents. But I want somebody to be there to control me, because people that have freedom want control, people that have control want freedom. We always want because we're human.

I don't really have regrets because it's all led me up to here. I like that I've had so much freedom to learn.

Maybe I'm looking for something to tell me what to believe, what're my limits. I don't know how it's going to end up. I'm kind of curious. Maybe I won't find it in religion. Maybe I'll find it in myself.

The Crucifix, the *Kippah*, and the Scarf

What does it mean to be a Christian? What does it mean to be a Jew? What does it mean to be a Muslim?

There are many answers to these questions. Although core beliefs unite the people within each of these faiths, each religion also has a wide variety of beliefs, practices, and philosophies. Splits within each faith are as wide as the gaps between any two of them.

On the following pages, Christians, Jews, and Muslims talk about their religious identities. They discuss some of the things that unite as well as divide them.

Certain garments and objects—the Christian crucifix, the Jewish kippah or skullcap, the Muslim hijab *or headscarf, for example—are powerful symbols of religious affiliation. These icons can bolster a person's faith and strengthen religious identity. But they can also force people to confront feelings of ambivalence and discomfort from others—and even from themselves.*

I Wanted to Make Sure I Wasn't Hiding Anything

Maureen, 20
Christian

I got this crucifix for confirmation from my mom, but I don't think I wore it. A lot of that was about me feeling uncomfortable about being a Christian.

I made a conscious decision to put it on last year because I was dealing with the whole identity-issue thing. It was me saying, "No, this is really silly. I should not be uncomfortable about it."

In putting it on, I was daring myself to do it, forcing myself to be out about it, because I knew that I was going to have a tendency to be shy about it. I put it on because I wanted to make sure I wasn't hiding anything.

It's also just a good reminder that I am not alone—that God is there for me.

It Takes a Lot of Courage to Wear a Kippah

Dan, 21
Jewish

When I was in high school, one of my friends was wearing a yarmulke,[2] and he was in the gym locker room and someone just grabbed it off his head and ran. In high school, teenagers are immature, ignorant, whatever.

---

[2] Yarmulke and kippah refer to the skullcap worn by many religious Jewish males.

I admire people who wear yarmulkes publicly. It's a courageous thing to do. Wearing it is a way for someone to say, "I'm a Jew." It's the biggest symbol. People who wear yarmulkes are generally more observant. For some kids who grow up in observant households, since day one they wear a kippah. So the thought never enters their minds that they cannot wear a kippah. But for a small minority out there, it's something they do as a way of showing Jewish pride.

I have friends who used to not wear them, and in their teenage years they said, "This is something I want to do." It's tough for someone to make that jump. I have a friend who used to go around wearing a baseball cap. You can wear a baseball cap—that counts as a yarmulke. Then he said, "You know what? I'm Jewish. I'm proud to be Jewish." So now he wears a kippah.

Especially if you're in a public forum, wearing a kippah requires a lot of courage, and you have to have a lot of pride in your religion. Some people in the business or professional worlds won't wear a kippah, because, unfortunately, a bit of anti-Semitism and prejudice exist there. U.S. Senator Joe Lieberman is the standard in that sense. I'm under the impression that he is observant. He doesn't wear a yarmulke. For some people in the professional world, it changes the way that people think of them, and perceptions are important.

Every once in a while, I think, "Maybe I should do it." I think I've ultimately never had the courage. The reason it's difficult, at least for myself in a tolerant community like this one, is that there's the fear—you don't want to stick out. But also, I'm satisfied with the level of my observance right now. Wearing a kippah is not the only way of making a statement of Jewish pride.

I Wanted to Revolutionize Myself from the Outside In

Sameera, 21
Muslim

I applied for a job in a pharmacy at a hospital. I'm trying to get into pharm school. They talked to me over the phone, and they were really excited. And when I went there and they saw that I wore the scarf, they were like, "We'll call you." And they didn't call me.

13

I called them to see what was happening, and they were like, "We're still interviewing people, we'll let you know." It's been going on for a couple of months, and I'm taking the hint they didn't like the fact that I wore hijab. I just got that vibe. They knew I was Muslim, but they didn't know how Muslim I was, I guess. I wear this, and I'm not going to take it off for any reason.

I started wearing hijab two years ago. Before that, I had been thinking about wearing it, but I was like, "I have plenty of time." Then something happened. I commuted by train, and a guy killed himself—he walked in front of our train. That got me thinking. Life is very fleeting, and you never know when you're going to die.

At that time, my Islam wasn't very strong, and I wanted to become a stronger person. A lot of people start inside to revolutionize themselves. I wanted to revolutionize myself from the outside in. That's why I started to wear hijab. It represents Islam. It made me connect with Allah, God. It made me more aware of Islam, of the necessary things that we have to do—prayer five times a day, fasting the whole month of Ramadan, giving charity to the poor, making a pilgrimage to the House of God if we have the means to do so, and reading and understanding the Qur'an. Islam is a way of life.

I went to a *Zabiha* meat store on Devon Avenue.[3] The Muslim community, especially Indians and Pakistanis, go there to shop for food, clothing, and to go to restaurants. And as we were waiting for our meat, I caught a glimpse of a bumper sticker that said, "Hijab is a symbol of modesty." **Wearing the scarf isn't just for covering the hair. It's a way of presenting yourself, a way of interacting with others in society—the type of clothing we wear, the way we act, and the way we speak to one another.**

We are taught when we are very young that we should live modestly and humble ourselves to God. Everything that we do is with thoughts of pleasing God. In Islam, there shouldn't be any vanity or pride. Guys think that it only applies to the girls, since we wear the scarf that ultimately shows that we are Muslim. But it also applies to them.

---

[3] Zabiha meats are from animals that have been slaughtered under restricted conditions.

What does it mean to be a Jew? Does it mean you practice the religion— Judaism? Does it mean one or both of your parents identify as Jews? Does it refer to your cultural heritage? Does it mean you're linked to a historical experience?

The issue of Jewish identity is complex and controversial. One reason is that a growing number of Americans, including a large segment of the Jewish-American community, is nonreligious or secular. Almost one out of three people who report Jewish parentage or upbringing is nonreligious.[4] This group doesn't participate in religious life or attend temple or synagogue.

The rising rate of interfaith marriage also has sparked debate about Jewish identity.

On the following pages, you'll hear from two religious Jews—a Reform Jew and an Orthodox Jew. You'll see that even among religious Jews, finding common ground can be challenging.

The Focus Is on Choice Through Knowledge

Abra, 20
Jewish (Reform)

I've heard that in Islam, someone's considered a Muslim if he publicly declares himself to be a Muslim. But in Judaism, how you become a Jew depends on which denomination you ask. If you ask someone from the Reform movement, somebody is Jewish if one parent is Jewish. If you ask someone from the Conservative or Orthodox movements, somebody is Jewish if their mother is Jewish. So we understand Jewish identity to be something that you're born with.

I was raised Reform. I belong to a Reform synagogue. My parents—one of them was raised Conservative, the other Reform.[5] We lit candles every Friday night to celebrate the Jewish Sabbath—it's from Friday at sundown to Saturday at sundown.

---

[4] This statistic is from the 2001 American Jewish Identity Survey, produced by the City University of New York's Center for Jewish Studies.

[5] In the Orthodox to Reform spectrum that many Jews use to describe their level of religious observance, Conservative falls in the middle.

Within Judaism there are three main denominations. Orthodox Judaism is the most traditional and observes the most rituals. Depending on how traditional they are, a lot of the time you can tell just from looking at someone that he's an Orthodox Jew. Orthodox women wear long skirts, wear shirts with sleeves that at least reach to the elbow, and cover their hair with a wig or a scarf.

Men may wear kipot skullcaps. They wear tefillin, which is like a white vest with fringes on four sides; you wear it under your clothes, so that's why you might see men with fringes hanging out of their shirts. Ultra-Orthodox men even wear black hats and black robes. Orthodox Jews don't drive or do work on the Sabbath. They don't turn on lights, don't answer the phone.

Reform Judaism is a different way of Jewish observance. It's more personal, because its main tenets are focused around choice through knowledge. We're the branch of Judaism that's less likely to prohibit driving on the Sabbath. But we also have the reputation for being the movement with the most commitment to social justice. We're most likely to be out there lobbying, doing community service, that type of thing. In Israel, Reform Judaism is not recognized as a valid denomination. We're not considered Jews. We can't even get married there.

If you're Conservative or Orthodox, most likely you'll keep kosher because you were raised that way. Part of keeping kosher means that Jews don't eat milk and meat together—there's a verse in the Torah about never eating a calf with its mother's milk. In Reform Judaism, if you find people who keep kosher, it's because it's their choice. You look into which of the Jewish laws you think are important and spiritual for your life, and you adopt those.

Choices

I spent the second semester of my junior year of high school in Israel, on North American Federation of Temple Youth's Eisendrath International Exchange. I was so moved by having this experience of learning the history of the Jews that I wanted to be able to incorporate something else into my life that could remind me of my Jewish identity on a daily basis. So I separated the dishes in my house according to "milk" or "meat." Luckily, we had two sets of dishes already, so we just separated them into two different cupboards. We separated our silverware, too, into different drawers for milk and meat.

My parents were like, "OK, cool, if you want to do that." After I separated the dishes, I was like, "Wait a minute, I can't have milk and meat together. Forget meat—I don't really like it or eat it that much, anyway." So I became vegetarian, and I've been vegetarian for two-and-a-half years. That's how I keep kosher.

Now it's a pretty big part of my life, and it dictates a lot of the choices I make. I definitely think I'm involved in social justice and political activism because of my motivations from Jewish templates. A Jewish code of ethics or righteousness shapes what I think about the value of a human being or the direction I should be taking in my life.

I also think it steers me in deciding who my community is going to be. That's important when you're at college—it's a big place, and you're trying to make friends to have some sort of community.

Judaism Is Always Available to You

It's my personal opinion that if you're born with it, even if you don't live your life as a Jew, Judaism's always available to you. You can learn more about it, and become involved, and have it become an important part of yourself. That's partly why Jews can go through periods of time when they're questioning, doubting God, doubting God's existence, but it's OK.

For such a long time, Jewish people have called themselves "People of Israel." The word Israel relates back to the story of Jacob wrestling with the angel. After Jacob defeated the angel, the angel granted him a new name— "Israel." In Hebrew, "Israel" means "he who struggles with God." So we're a people who define our identity by the fact that we are always struggling with God.

A Combined Set of Practices and Beliefs

Lena,* 22
Jewish (Orthodox)
*not her real name

There are a lot of internal identity politics about what it means to be Orthodox. People have said to me, when I talk about theology, particularly, "I don't know how you can call yourself an Orthodox Jew if you don't think . . . blah blah blah."

If you're Orthodox, you see all the [Jewish religious] laws as binding. But there are about five people in the world who keep everything. For most people, the ideal and the real are different, at least to some extent.

There are a lot of people who would look at anyone who came to the university and go, "They're not really Orthodox." I definitely fall into that category by virtue of having a secular education and having gone to a coed high school. Unlike a lot of coed high schools, girls and boys actually had everything together, except for gym. There aren't many modern Orthodox schools where they do that.

If I was "really Orthodox," I would have gone to a separate-sex high school, and then I would have gone to either a Jewish college or a community college, and then gotten married. A girl who is twenty-two, living alone in an apartment, hanging out with non-Jews, and not caring about being not married is already sort of problematic. And I study philosophy, which is quasi-heretical.

So I'm sort of Orthodox, in the sense that people have also bought into the idea of Orthodox as a set of beliefs—meaning that you buy into the Orthodox system, which I do—that halachic authority, Halachah being Jewish law, is ultimately Orthodox and not non-Orthodox. For an Orthodox Jew, only Orthodox rabbis have authority. Conservative rabbis can't tell *me* what's OK or what's not OK.

What keeps Orthodox Judaism together is a combined set of practices and beliefs. Obviously there are people with widely different beliefs, but the system is based on the same sort of authority structure, the same set of canonized texts. And you have to learn these in order to be able to interpret them.

There are lots of non-Orthodox for whom being Jewish is a real part of their identity, and they struggle with questions, and that's great. But there are a lot of people who don't.

I think in the beginnings of the Reform, the Conservative, and the Reconstructionist movements,[6] there were people who had traditional educations, knew a lot, and just couldn't stand the way things were going under Orthodoxy. They felt like they had to change it. And the challenge has been to perpetuate that sense of commitment.

The laity of these movements, and even of the left wing of Orthodoxy, can sometimes be like, "I'm Conservative (or Reform, or modern . . .), so I don't

---

[6] The Reconstructionist movement is the youngest of the major Jewish movements or denominations.

have to care as much," as opposed to, like, "I'm Conservative or . . . , so I have to care and exercise really painful choices between tradition and my modern tendencies." The challenge is to keep the questions of tradition alive once you're no longer practicing it or focusing on it as much.

With a lot of people who identify as Reform—what they mean is like, "I'm Jewish every once in a while. Sometimes I go home and we have Passover. And it doesn't mean that I subscribe to this whole idea of Jewish identity or any sort of religiosity. It just means that I'm less Jewish than those Orthodox people."

There are a lot of people who are serious Reform or Conservative Jews, but there is definitely an undercurrent in secular unaffiliated American Judaism where people who don't know so much about what's going on will say, "There are levels in Judaism. The Orthodox are most Jewish. And the Reform are people like me who do whatever we want but are still Jewish." I find that approach sort of silly.

One of the most obvious divisions among the Christians I interviewed was the rift between the Christian right—primarily made up of fundamentalist and evangelical Christians—and mainline and progressive Christians.

Among most of the fundamentalists and evangelicals I spoke with, faith is rooted in the absolute conviction that Jesus Christ is the savior of all humanity. The only path to salvation, they believe, is through acceptance of Christ.

Only One Way to Heaven

Julie,* 20
Christian (nondenominational)
*not her real name

My father is not Christian, he doesn't believe in God the way I do. He's Catholic, he goes to church, but I don't think he believes all the things the Catholic Church does. I know the Catholic Church teaches there's only one God. He doesn't believe in one God. He believes that Allah is God, whoever you want to worship is God—it's your own choice. I hate to make the Christian faith sound unbending, but there is only one God, only one way to heaven.

I don't believe that a church affiliation saves you. I think that you become saved by accepting Jesus Christ as your savior, and you believe in him and he gives you the desire to follow him. You do your best to live a good upright life.

But obviously we're all human. So being Christian doesn't guarantee that you're gonna never sin.

None of us deserves to go to heaven. But God, in his mercy, sent his only son to take our sins on himself. When people reject his son, it's like a slap in his face. Jesus himself said, "I'm the only way. No man can come to the father except by me."

It's unbending, but it's just the way it is.

Julie's views were echoed by other conservative Christians I spoke with. However, many Christians—both Catholics and Protestants—were not as rigid. Anthony was one of these people.

Am I Still Catholic? Yes, I Am.

Anthony, 23
Christian (Catholic)

I'm from Beaumont, Texas. My dad grew up Catholic. My mom was a Southern Baptist before she married my dad. She was really active in the Baptists when she was younger. She was in choir and traveled all over the country.

She became Catholic because of the craziness that happened when they got married. Her minister said, "You're making the biggest mistake of your life," because my father was Catholic. He was trying to convince her to go into the military instead. She was like, "No, I love the guy."

They had the wedding at the Catholic church, and the minister was supposed to come, and he didn't come. And they had the reception at her place of worship, and he didn't come there. But the Catholic priest came. After that she became Catholic.

My mom is a more liberal person than my dad, but my mom is a more fanatical Catholic. So every Sunday we went to seven o'clock mass, early in the morning. It was like clockwork. Usually it was me, my brother, and my mom going to mass, and if my dad was off work, he would go to mass. At my house, mass was always important, holy days were always important. We'd go to mass before school; that was our obligation.

I was an altar boy. I started at seven or eight and went all the way until high school. I went to Catholic school all my life. I was one of three or four black kids in the class.

I participated in CYO, Catholic Youth Organization, in junior high. There was a board of eight youths in CYO who planned all the service and social events at the diocese level. I was on that board for two years. **CYO was the only thing that kept me in Catholicism. I saw fellowship happening, I saw people doing things for people—I thought, this is what Christianity is about. I didn't get that out of mass or just reading the Bible.**

I went to high school, the only private school in town. It was a Catholic school, but it was very different than most Catholic schools. It was only about 50 percent Catholic. It was more interfaith. We had a lot more prayer services than masses. We had an ecumenical prayer service every year. All the different religions that were represented at my school would send some religious leader to come to that service.

I went to a Jesuit university, Loyola in New Orleans. The Jesuits are an order in the Catholic Church, but they are very liberal. They were kicked out of the Catholic Church a couple times because of their beliefs. I've become a lot more liberal and on that socially active kind of mind train.

Maybe Loyola students were more critical of Catholicism because we were taught to look at religion in critical ways. We separated our Bible of literature from our Bible of faith. We can look at the Bible and say, "Maybe this didn't really happen—but the idea is still there." Or "Maybe this is not saying we should hate these people—this is someone twisting something around." There's a bigger truth to the Bible, and good things that might help you live a better life. You can look at something from an educational standpoint and it doesn't have to destroy your faith viewpoint, it can help enforce it. That's something that Jesuits are very much about.

Being Catholic

I still see myself as being very Catholic. I do hold the tenets of the Catholic Church—the idea that Jesus was God. My actions, the things that I say, or how I live my life—am I still Catholic? Yes, I am, because I feel that Catholicism has given me the morals that I need, and my conscience is acting out of what I think is right. Therefore, I'm still being Catholic, even though I might not agree with what the pope says or what my local priest says. My ideas are very different from mainstream Catholicism. I don't think priests have a special power. I think the holy order is tapped by God to be leaders.

The church of my dad is a little different from mine and the one that my mom converted to. Vatican II in the '60s changed a lot.[7] After Vatican II the mass would be said in vernacular language and not in Latin anymore. The Second Vatican Council made a lot of statements as far as what it means to be Catholic. It said that we are not the only church and established the ecumenical idea that we do see other religions as valid. It made the clear statement that Jews were not the killers of Christ and, therefore, we do not see them as condemned forever to hell. And there's the idea that if you're not Catholic, you're not going to be damned to hell. A lot of people were unhappy with that and left the church.

Some of those things are just now starting to change. Religious change happens last, way behind society, because there's so much that has to be altered to make it fit. How long did it take for people to be OK with a small thing like women being altar servers in the Catholic Church? People were like, "What's going on? That's nuts!" In my parish it didn't happen until 1989.

I couldn't be Catholic without a statement like Vatican II. The idea behind it is that you do what your conscience tells you to do and that overrides everything—be it a papal decree, be it what your priest says.

I think Vatican II is something that set a big ball into motion. I think a hundred years from now the church is going to be completely different. I'm sad to say it, but certain people who are in control and in power all over the world will have to give that power to younger people who are growing up in these societies where the social change is happening.

---

[7] The Second Vatican Council, or Vatican II, was a gathering of Roman Catholic officials that occurred each autumn from 1962 through 1965.

I feel it's my duty, other lay people's duty, and the priests' duty to make things more what they should be. Yeah, it is wrong for priests to molest people. But no way does it mean I'm going to leave the Catholic Church. I'm going to find some way to right what's wrong.

They Don't Consider Us Muslims

Qasim, 20
Muslim (Ahmadi)

I was born an Ahmadi Muslim. We're a sect of Islam. The Ahmadiyya Movement was founded by a man named Hadhrat Mirza Ghulam Ahmad. He was born in 1835 and passed away in 1908. We believe him to be the divine reformer sent by God to unite mankind as one. His mission was to unite all religions and guide mankind to Allah under the comprehensive religion of Islam. He is the messiah. Because of this belief, we've been ousted by the entire Muslim community. They don't consider us Muslims.

There's a group of Muslims that get together and pass something called a *fatwa*, like a decree. They passed a fatwa that we are not Muslim because we don't believe that Muhammad, peace be upon him, was the last prophet. They passed a fatwa that we're not Muslims because we don't believe that Jesus is going to physically descend from heaven. Many Muslims believe that Jesus is alive in heaven right now and is going to come down one day.

On April 26, 1984, an ordinance was introduced to the Pakistani constitution and made it a criminal offense for Ahmadis to call themselves Muslim, to use Muslim places of worship—such as mosques—to use Muslim terminology, or to propagate their faith. One section states that anyone declaring Prophet Muhammad(saw) as not the last prophet,[8] as Ahmadis believe, will be sentenced to death.

---

[8] After the Prophet Muhammad, the abbreviation "(saw)" or "(pbuh)" is written. SAW stands for "sullullah wa alaihi wa salaam." This translates into "May the peace and blessings of God be upon him," hence PBUH.

Islamic Interfaith

We had an interfaith discussion between Sunni Muslims and Ahmadi Muslims.[9] Afterwards, me and my brother were talking to a few Sunni Muslims. We were discussing whether or not Muhammad, peace be upon him, was the last prophet. And we pointed out a verse that said categorically he was not. One of the guys was like, "You know what? It doesn't matter, because you're a kafir." He was calling us insults right and left and raising his voice.

In all honesty, a Muslim has no right to call another Muslim a non-Muslim. In the Qur'an, Allah tells the Prophet Muhammad, peace be upon him, do not call anybody a non-Muslim—the Arabic word for it is "kafir" or disbeliever—because you don't know what's in their heart, only God knows that.

It hurts me to realize that there are some Sunni Muslims out there who would not consider me a Muslim simply because of my beliefs. But I'll call them Muslims because they believe in God; they believe in the Day of Judgment; they do good things for poor people.

It's expected. When Christ came to the Jews, they rejected him. When Prophet Muhammad, peace be upon him, came, the first people who rejected him were the Meccans of Arabia. There has never been a time when a prophet has come and has been accepted right away. They've all had to face persecution. This is part of human nature. But as time passed, they were accepted. It doesn't surprise us that we're being persecuted.

We've seen some issues that divide believers within a faith. One out of four American adults is Roman Catholic, according to the 2001 American Religious Identification Survey produced by the Graduate Center of the City University of New York. This makes Catholicism the largest Christian denomination in this country. They're an amazingly diverse group of people. So what ties Roman Catholics together? For sixteen-year-old Maggie, the answer is the pope, the leader of the Roman Catholic Church.

The chance to see current Pope John Paul II caused an estimated 200,000 young people from around the globe to converge on Toronto, Canada, in July 2002 for World Youth Day.

---

[9] The majority of Muslims in the U.S. and in the world are Sunni Muslims.

He's Like the Knot in Catholicism

Maggie, 16
Christian (Catholic)

Seeing the pope was just amazing. You see him on TV, but when you actually get to see him—I was in total awe. He's very frail. He's very sick. But his cheeks were red, and he was smiling. He waved. He looked alive for World Youth Day and happy to be there.

He talked to us. He was like, "You guys have to spread the word of Catholicism to everybody and show them how important it is to you." And you can tell that he has so much faith in what youth are doing and how we can bring up the Catholic Church. I expected that it was going to be emotional. I didn't know that it was going to impact me that much.

There was a stage and a path leading up to the stage, through the crowd. We were right by the path where we could see him. We were there for five hours waiting. Everybody around me was crying when he came by, and I was, too. We were from different countries, and everyone was speaking different languages. He speaks all those languages, and he has so much religion in him. He's what ties us all together. He's like the knot in Catholicism.

I feel my religion is much more important to me than before I went. Before I went there, I went to mass, I got confirmed, I was doing all the steps to be Catholic, but I just didn't feel it. My friends always asked me questions about my religion. And so now I feel that if they do ask me a question, I can share with them what I experienced at World Youth Day. It was life changing.

Sometimes a person—the pope in the case of Roman Catholics—can ignite spiritual passion and forge a sense of religious community and identity. Certain places also hold tremendous spiritual power. For Jews, Christians, and Muslims, many of these places are located in the Middle East, the shared birthplace of their religions.

Observant Muslims pray five times a day. Each time, they turn to face Mecca, Saudi Arabia, the holiest city in Islam. Nineteen-year-old Arif describes a pilgrimage to Mecca.

You Imagine the Prophet Is There

Arif, 19
Muslim

We pray five times a day toward the Ka'ba, or toward Mecca. The Ka'ba itself is just like a big cube. Nothing is inside it. According to the Qur'an, the Ka'ba was built by Abraham and his son Ismail. They built this house for the sole purpose of worshipping God. But the location, the land around it, is declared holy by God and in the Qur'an. So we pray toward that land.

Many unknowledgeable people have the idea that we are worshipping an idol. However, the reason why we pray in that direction is not because the Ka'ba is an idol. In fact, before we started praying toward the Ka'ba, we were praying toward Jerusalem.

You can see the wisdom in the fact that God sent down one particular place for everyone to pray toward. You can see an idea of unity. **And if you look at the religion of Islam, everything is one. You have one god, one last prophet, one Qur'an—and you have one place where you pray toward, as well. So this idea of unity, the idea of oneness—it's a symbolic feature of that.**

For seventeen years I was praying toward this area, the Ka'ba, and I didn't know anything about it. The first time I went there was when I was seventeen. I went over with a number of youth to do 'umra and to study a little bit, memorize Qur'an. The 'umra is a spiritual journey to Mecca you can take at any time. The hajj is a pilgrimage to the House of God, Ka'ba. The hajj is obligatory— Muslims have to do it once in their lives at least, if they are financially and physically able. It's at a prescribed time of the year. I haven't done it yet.

When you go for 'umra, there's two main things you need to do. You need to do a circumambulation around the Ka'ba seven times.[10] During that time you make supplications and prayers to God.

Islamic Pilgrimage

There were thousands. On Fridays you will find between 500,000 to a million people there. You see everyone from different areas. You'll see Indonesian people there. You'll see Chinese people there, Pakistani, Indians, Africans, and Americans, as well. The idea of community is instilled in your head when you go visit. All the men must put on two white sheets known as the ihram. And the women must wear their hijab. The purpose of wearing the ihram is to show the idea of simplicity and humbleness and a sense of unity and equality.

You're walking, walking, and then slowly you see the Ka'ba come into view. And that's where you see the people doing the circumambulation. It's indescribable, the feeling you have. A lot of the youth I went with—tears started coming down.

You hear the *Adhan*, which is the call to prayer on the loud speakers. That experience in itself is another level of joy, because when you live in America, you only hear it in the *masjids* [mosques], and a lot of times not that well. But when it's ringing through the city, and you see crowds of people walking to the masjids, that's an experience in itself.

Then, there's two hills called Safa and Marwa. You have to walk toward Safa once, and Marwa once. You do this seven times. During that time you also make supplication and prayers to God.

The Bible and the Qur'an

According to the Qur'an, Abraham was told to leave Hagar—her name in Arabic is Hajar—in this area. He tells her to have trust in Allah, and he leaves. She has her young infant, Ismail, with her, and there is no water, and her son was starving and thirsty. So she runs to one hill, then she runs to the other hill, looking for caravans to come so she can get water. She does this seven times. And the water starts flowing beneath Ismail—it was basically mercy from God. So Safa and Marwa are symbolic of the fact that you have to trust in God. This is the short version of it.

---

[10] The circumambulation is done walking in a counterclockwise direction.

You'll see a similar story in the Bible, but it doesn't mention exactly where Abraham takes Hajar and Ismail. If you look in the Bible and the Qur'an, you'll see very similar stories. You'll see stories about Abraham, you'll see stories about Noah, you'll see stories about Lot, and stories about all the prophets beforehand. However, the Qur'anic version may be a little bit different from the Biblical version; there may be additions or subtractions. The Qur'an is not a storybook. These stories of the past in the Qur'an give you lessons that you can implement in your life.

When you go there, you imagine the Prophet is there, you imagine his companions are there, you imagine different events in the Prophet's life. When you come back, the images are not out of your mind. When you come back, you can visualize that experience when you're praying *salat*.

Basically, everything is intertwined in the religion of Islam. There are the five Pillars of Islam: the *shahadah*,[11] or coming into Islam; salat, which is the five daily prayers; and then *zakat*, giving alms; the observance of the month of Ramadan; and lastly the hajj.

When you go to the hajj or you go to the 'umra, it increases the effectiveness of your five daily prayers. It's a very different experience when you go there in person and you see the Ka'ba in front of you, and you see the brotherhood in front of you, and you see the idea of an Islamic community. It's an amazing experience.

Israel is the nexus of Jewish identity for many American Jews, religious and secular alike. According to the Old Testament, the land that is now Israel was the birthplace of Judaism and the home of the Jewish people. In 1948 the state of Israel was created.

Each year, thousands of Jewish-American teenagers and young adults visit the country to renew their faith and to learn about Jewish history. In the summer of 2002, Rebecca went on a trip that was organized by United Synagogue Youth. She and a group of Jewish teenagers also visited some sites in Europe where many Jews were killed during the Holocaust. Throughout Europe, six million Jews perished at the hands of the Nazis during World War II. For Rebecca, the pilgrimage clarified and fortified her identity as a Jew. Here's an excerpt from the journal she kept.

---

[11] The shahadah is a confession of faith: "There is no god but God, and Muhammad is His Prophet."

Being Jewish Is about Learning from Our History

Rebecca, 17
Jewish (Conservative)

Sunday June 30, 2002

I'm now sitting inside Treblinka where the train tracks used to be. It hasn't truly hit me yet where I am. The place looks empty now—it's hard to imagine the gas chambers, mass murder, and depression that were once here. We just heard the song "The Little Station Treblinka." It sounds like a train and speaks of getting off the train at the Treblinka station, the station of death. We now split up to walk amongst the rocks in the memorial. There are 17,000 memorial stones to represent the killing capacity of the gas chambers, which was 17,000 per day. Some of the stones have names written on them of Jewish communities that were exterminated or involved in the Holocaust somehow.

I took a candle and placed it next to a stone that says Stopnica on it. I wanted to look if there was a stone with Shepetovka on it, the city where my grandpa's family was from, but there are too many stones to look for just one, especially since it probably isn't even here. I don't know why I picked this stone with the name Stopnica on it, but I did. I hope that in Israel or at home I'll be able to learn more about this community to make it personal.

At Treblinka here, all is silent except for the chirping of the birds. I had always imagined the death camps as gray and desolate, but everything here is green. The forest surrounding the camp is lush and bright—it doesn't seem to fit with the depression and tragedy that characterize Treblinka.

Walking around and seeing the names of the lost communities, I feel so fortunate, so lucky to live in a thriving Jewish community. **And it makes my job and our job much clearer—we must continue the legacy of the Jewish people. We must show our fellow Jews that these communities were lost but we still live on, and we, the Jewish people, will live on forever.** More than ever, I now truly realize why the Land of Israel is so important. With our homeland in Israel, we know that Jewish communities will never again be exterminated—

we have a place to go, a homeland that will welcome us with open arms. If only the thousands of Jews who died here each day also had somewhere to go.

By going on a pilgrimage from here to Israel we are symbolically representing the transition from the Holocaust to our state of Israel, our Jewish homeland. Being Jewish is about our connection—our connection to all Jews around the world—past, present, and future. Being Jewish is about the connection I feel to the communities engraved upon these rocks and the connection to them through determination to preserve their legacy. It's about the connection I just established with the Jewish community of Stopnica. Being Jewish is about learning from our history and working together *k'am echad*—as one nation—to preserve the beauty of our tradition and ensure that such a tragedy happens never again.

As I stood here among the sorrow, thinking about being Jewish, I felt the sudden need to affirm my commitment and belief in G-d. I stood in the midst of the memorial rocks, facing out toward the green forest, and uttered the words of the *Shema* in Hebrew:[12]

> *Sh'ma yisrael Adonai Eloheinu Adonai ehad.*
> *Ehad Eloheinu, gadol Adoneinu, kadosh sh'mo.*
> Hear, O Israel: The Lord our G-d, the Lord is one.
> One is our G-d, great our Lord, holiness is His nature.

I got choked up and began to tear as I uttered these words of faith. I didn't full out cry, but it was hard to speak because I was so choked up and the tears began to form in my eyes. Never before was it so hard to utter these words, but never before did I say them with such meaning and pride. Standing in a place where hundreds of thousands of Jews were murdered, I was able to declare that I still believed in G-d and his righteousness in ruling over the world. I did question how G-d could let such tragedy and horror occur—and this question will never be answered. I have learned to accept that, and it felt comforting to utter the Shema, to utter my faith in G-d forever.

As I walked back to the big monument, we had a memorial service together, which was very moving, but I didn't cry. I always cry when I'm alone . . .

---

[12] Shema, which is recited several times a day, is a proclamation of faith in God.

maybe I just deal with these things in a personal way and would rather deal with them alone when I can really think by myself. As we walked out of Treblinka together, the sun immediately started to come out. This really struck me as significant—it really hit me and gave me hope that things will be OK and life does go on.

Another thing that struck me as beautiful was the way our group held together and supported each other. I saw people giving each other hugs, putting their arms around each other, and asking if everyone was OK. I really saw everyone come together . . . this is making our bond even stronger.

Interfaith relationships are especially common and controversial among Jewish-Americans. Half of all the Jewish-Americans who married since 1990 married a non-Jewish spouse, according to the 2001 American Jewish Identity Survey produced by the City University of New York's Center for Jewish Studies. In this survey, Jews were those who said they were Jewish by religion, by parentage, or by upbringing.

Should the child of Jewish and Christian parents choose the religious identity of one parent over the other? Is it possible for a family to embrace the faiths of both parents? Two teenagers found different answers to these questions.

I Wear Two Stars of David

Sara, 18
Jewish (Reform)

I wear two Stars of David. My brother gave me one for my bat mitzvah. The other one—me and my friend decided we were going to have bat mitzvahs together and that was her present to me. I haven't taken them off since I was thirteen.

I like it when people know that I'm Jewish. I don't wear a kippah or a big sign that says "I'm Jewish." But this is my little way of letting people know, especially since I don't look Jewish. There are some people, you just look at them and assume they're Jewish. They look a certain way. I don't look anything like a Jew. So it's sort of my way of saying "I'm Jewish"—like a little sign.

It kind of annoys me when people say, "You can't be Jewish because you have blond hair and blue eyes." There's a million Jews with blond hair and blue eyes, but there's that stereotype of dark curly hair, big nose, brown eyes. My mom has the brown hair. She doesn't have really stereotypical Jewish features, but she looks more Jewish than I do. I don't look anything like my mom.

Me and my brother both look like my dad. His background is Irish, Scottish, Welsh, and German. My brother's friends call him the "Viking Jew" because he has white blond hair; he wears it in a ponytail. He's really big, like 6' 3" and 200-something pounds. We both look very not-Jewish, so that's what I hear more about than anything else.

It's always been very clear to me that I was Jewish. That's always been a really clear part of my identity. My dad was Methodist. When he was growing up, they went to church every once in a while, but they were never really religious. They didn't get mad when he said he converted to Judaism. He converted when I was ten, right before my brother's bar mitzvah. So he knows very little about anything Jewish.

My mom has always been Jewish, but she grew up in a very, very secular household. They lived in Milwaukee and during the time period when she was growing up, it was sort of hush-hush if you were Jewish, and her parents didn't want to say anything. So she didn't know very much, either.

I think it's really important to have an identity. You can't be both. I think that's really stupid, confusing for kids. They'll think, "What am I?" You have to pick one or the other. That's the point of a religion—you believe in something, you give part of yourself to something. You can't give half yourself to this religion and half yourself to that religion. Then, it doesn't mean anything.

I feel really connected with my Jewish community, but a little less connected to the observance factor of my religion. I don't keep kosher. I don't really feel that that's necessary. When I was little, my whole family would sit down every Friday night and light the *Shabbat* candles and say the blessings. We don't do that anymore. Now it's like, "It's Friday night. I'm going to go out with my friends."

I don't like organized prayer. Every once in a while I go to services, but I appreciate it a lot more when I do my own thing and say my own prayers. I don't think it takes an hour-and-a-half or two hours to say what I want to say to God. Sometimes I feel like I should celebrate Shabbat more. But then I feel that if I did do that, I'd never see my friends.

A lot of my friends at school are Jewish by birth, but they stopped going to synagogue when they were like eight, or they have never been to synagogue. They don't believe in anything, they're anti–organized religion. They're like, "I'm not Jewish." I'm like, "Yeah, you are."

According to Jewish law, if your mother is Jewish, then you are Jewish, and that's that. You can't get away from it. You can become a priest, and you're still Jewish. To me, they're all Jewish. And to them, they're not. They say they're culturally Jewish but not anything else.

When I was younger, I never really thought I was different 'cause I was Jewish. It didn't occur to me until high school when I started getting really involved with stuff. It's kind of weird when I really think about it. It's like I'm just like everyone else, except there's that little part of me that's going to be Jewish forever, and that makes me different.

"How Can You Be Both?"

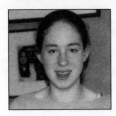

Nora, 16
Interfaith Family (Jewish and Christian)

My mother is Catholic, and my father is Jewish—he was actually raised Orthodox and then fell away from the faith. Then he started dating my mom. They were married by a rabbi, and he got back into going to synagogue. So I was raised both.

I went to Catholic school and had religious ed. Until January of the seventh grade, I was what was called a "shooting star"—a person of any faith besides Roman Catholic. Then I came to the conclusion that I believed more what the Catholics believe—the Jesus-is-God thing. So I was confirmed Catholic. I was thirteen.

When I graduated and went into the eighth grade, I went to public school. I miss the religious ed. But I've found amazing friendships at Lincoln Park High School. It's funny because there are so many of us there who care deeply about our faith lives. I don't think many teenagers take the time to think about where they are in regards to God.

Religion is very, very present in my life. We go to church every Sunday. If I don't go to church on Sunday, something is wrong in the world. My church, Old St. Patrick's on the West Side, is like my second home. We've been going for ten years, so I know a lot of people there. My parents are very active within the community.

It's such an amazing, amazing place. It's very welcoming. It's very liberal. They don't deal with any of that crap—like the doctrines of the church. So it's not one of the cardinal's favorite churches in Chicago.

It's probably the only church where they'll print things constantly about Jewish holidays. There was something last week in the bulletin about Holocaust Remembrance Day. We had Peace Week last week, and they gave us this slip of paper that had this peace prayer on it, and it also had the Jewish prayer for peace on the back.

Our synagogue is Sinai. It, too, is very ecumenical and very welcoming of interfaith families, which is interesting because so much of the Jewish community shuns interfaith families. They think that there are so few Jews to begin with, that if you marry a non-Jew, the chances are you won't raise your child Jewish and they'll lose even more potential congregants. Many rabbis won't do interfaith weddings, but Sinai does.

I also was going to Sunday-school classes—it's called Family School. My parents helped start it about ten years ago for children of interfaith families. In Family School we'd talk a lot about Judaism and Catholicism and social situations that would come up. We'd talk about scenarios where our peers would be curious and ask.

I've had instances when people, peers of mine, will tell me that I'm not really Jewish because my mother is not the Jewish one. "How can you be both? You can't be two religions, especially Catholicism and Judaism." It happens to be a guy who is of the Jewish faith who says these things to me. And I tend to become very defensive about it. I think he's curious. We'll sit down and have a conversation about it. I can help enlighten him because of my experience of being given all this valuable information about these faiths.

The Jesus Question

There is one very large issue, obviously, that Jews and Christians differ on, which is Jesus and the Holy Trinity. So there, I think you have to go one way or another. In my own faith life, I decided that this is my gut feeling: God said, "You people down there on Earth don't get it. So I have to show you how to be kind to each other and compassionate of one another." So he manifested himself in Jesus.

But what I've learned through the Family School is that Judaism and Catholicism are really similar in many ways. So much of Catholicism is taken from Judaism. I'll go to synagogue and we'll be reading things, and I'll be like, "We just sang that in a song on Sunday."

When I was going through my confirmation, I remember this man who is the faith formation guide at OSP [Old St. Patrick's], said, "If you want to lead a life of love, that's what confirmation is about—confirming a sense of leading this life of love."

I was just so taken with that, because I think so much of religion is labels.

Who cares if you're Catholic or you're Jewish or you're Baha'i or you're Buddhist or you're Muslim or whatever the heck you are. As long as you believe in something that makes sense to you, who cares what the rest of the world calls it?

I think there is a lot of fluidity in religion, and so much of one religion melds into another. All those titles, all those doctrines, are just man-made. Does God really care whether or not you go to church or kneel three times or say the rosary four times a day? No, I don't think he does.

There's a lot of things about the Catholic Church that I don't agree with—the whole hierarchy structure, the celibacy issue, that women can't be priests. But I do believe in Jesus and in being kind and compassionate to one another, which is a common thread through all religion. How to be a better human being—that's what's the most important thing. It doesn't matter what you call yourself.

Religious conflict can take place within a person as he or she grows within a faith.

My Identity As a Jew Is Always Changing

Jacob,* 15
Jewish (Reform)
*not his real name

My father's a rabbi. But I'm not the typical RK—rabbi's kid. Some RKs I know—they're just stuck up. They know that they own the place, basically. You can get kind of prissy and annoying. I try to be fair and accepting.

It's hard sometimes. You're always in the spotlight. When I went to Jewish school, everyone was like, "He's the rabbi's son. No wonder he's acing Jewish-studies class." But I learned just as much as everybody else from class.

When my friends find out, they're like, "Oh, you're the rabbi's kid. You must be very religious and very holier-than-thou." But I'm normal, Dad's normal. People don't realize sometimes that preachers and rabbis, they're normal people.

It's hard, too, because I don't want to look bad for my father. But I also have to remember that I'm not there just for him. Sometimes I wish I were just another member of the congregation, that I can just be at the synagogue and pray, as opposed to politicking—being nice to everybody and being friendly and making the rounds.

But I feel it's not as bad as people may think it is. I try to hold myself well in the synagogue. I think I'm very lucky—I like my father, I like my mother. Being a rabbi's kid can be hard sometimes, but I don't regret it at all.

We're more traditional than most Reform families. When you think of Reform, you think of somebody not keeping the Sabbath, where I keep it all of the time. I went to the Conservative day school, and I'm involved with the Conservative youth group. I just kind of mix.

I'll Always Be Changing

I don't think it's right to have one definitive thing that makes somebody Jewish. I don't think that's fair to do that to anybody. I think it's really important that the definition of Judaism be something you define for yourself. If you don't follow the laws but you try to be moral and just be a good person, then that's Jewish. Judaism teaches that you have to adapt to your time period—where you are and who you are.

I think my identity as a Jew is always changing. I don't think it will stop changing ever. I'm influenced by different things, different people. I see what they see and I think about where I stand and what I feel. I think I'm definitely now in a process where I have no idea exactly where I am. I have no idea exactly where I stand or who I am or anything of that nature.

But I think that's OK. I think that's what's really important—to just constantly evolve and keep getting better. I really like history and policy. I might want to go into politics. But I'm not afraid for that to change, too.

I think one good thing about Judaism is that it tries to get people to think for themselves. I find that Judaism is very individualistic, which is good. And I think that if you study Torah and you study the law, you'll find the answers that can help you with your problems. But sometimes that's hard, which is why we have rabbis to help.

Community

Another great thing about Judaism is that a big part of it is community—a great sense of community and a strong support system. You saw that with aid to Russia in the '80s and early '90s. U.S. Jewish organizations raised money to help support Russian Jews who could not freely identify themselves or leave the U.S.S.R. Support like this continues to this day as immigrants are moved to Israel or the U.S. Israel airlifted thousands of Ethiopian Jews out of Ethiopia to avoid persecution and brought them to Israel. We'll send money just because people are Jewish.

I believe that while individuals must have their own understanding of themselves as Jews, they must be a part of the Jewish community. Throughout Jewish literature, we see the importance of a holy community, *Kehillat Kedushah*. This is vital and necessary to the survival of Judaism.

You Can't Force Yourself to Be Ready to Believe

A former Catholic talks about her decision to leave the Catholic Church and how she found a spiritual home.

Maureen, 20
Christian

When I was growing up, a big part of Catholicism for me was my Irish heritage. Both my parents are Irish-American; my family has been here for generations. I didn't go to Catholic school or anything like that, and my church wasn't an Irish-American church—it was actually pretty diverse as Catholic churches go. But my devotion to Catholicism, as opposed to other forms of Christianity, was always more a cultural thing.

I was Catholic because being Catholic, instead of Protestant, was and is a big deal in Ireland and Northern Ireland. Being Catholic was my way of recognizing my past, my ancestors, and the problems that continue in Northern Ireland today. The history of violence there and what is going on now is really depressing. I'm going to go and work in Northern Ireland this summer for a human-rights organization.

But while it's important that I identify with and think about and try to do what I can to help things in Northern Ireland, it's also important to recognize that there are other places in the world that have it far worse. There are issues in Africa that are more life threatening than issues in Northern Ireland right now.

My dad's an ex–altar boy. He went from that to thinking that religion is the cause of the majority of the world's problems. So we didn't go to church growing up until my parents split up, which was when I was eight. And then my mom started bringing us to church almost right away.

We always did Christmas and Easter, but totally secularly for the most part. We always said prayer before dinner, but for me there was no meaning behind it. So even at eight, I didn't buy into the whole thing. I went through Sunday school and first communion, but I never really got into it or understood what was going on.

MY FAITH JOURNEY

I'm the Kind of Person Who Takes Things Seriously.

Then when I was about fourteen, I went through the whole confirmation process. At the time, I took it really seriously and was trying to figure out if this was something I actually wanted to do. I thought a lot about it. I decided that I wanted to do it. So I got confirmed. Within a year of that, I had a lot of anxiety over it because I realized I had a lot of issues with the whole Jesus thing—I didn't think it was very feasible.

I believed in God, but I didn't believe that Christ was God's son, sent here to save us. I thought he was a pretty cool guy. I thought he was like Martin Luther King—he was worthy of our honor and respect and he was a revolutionary in a lot of ways, but I wasn't sure that a religion should be formed around him. So I got to feeling uncomfortable going to church because I'm the kind of person who takes things seriously. **When you go up to get communion and the priest looks in your eyes and you're not buying it, it's a really bad feeling. So I stopped going to church.**

I remember having one altercation with my mom about it. It was Easter, and I thought to myself, "I'll go to church because it's a family thing, it's not that big of a deal." So I went to church with my mom, and the priest talked about how it was a holiday and there were more people than usual, referring to the "holiday Catholics."

My mom nudged me, and I got so mad—she seemed to think I didn't go to church because I was lazy, not because I had made a serious decision and didn't want to sit in church and lie about my beliefs. I just sat there infuriated through the rest of the service. I got home and went straight up to my room. She was like, "Is something wrong?"

I said, "Listen, Mom, me not going to church is a decision I made because I feel really uncomfortable when I'm there because I don't believe it. So unless you want me to lie by going to church, this is what I'm going to do." She was like, "Wow, that's a much better reason for not going to church than mine." After that, she was OK with it.

God As a Partner

Then my sister got married my first year in college, and it wasn't through the Catholic Church. I went home for her wedding, and it was really a powerful experience for me. My sister and her husband are very honest about their relationship with God and have a sincerity about Christianity that I had never seen before. They weren't just committing to themselves. They were bringing this third entity—God/Christ—in and saying, "We're coming together, but we're also coming together with you, and we know that, no matter what, you're going to make sure that we stay together." God has a distinct role in their marriage. It was amazing to me, especially coming from having divorced parents and always having doubts about marriage in general.

They lived in Chicago at the time. I started going to church with them. It was interesting because I didn't believe at the time. But I felt really comfortable, so I started going more and more often. There's a big difference, I feel, between Catholicism and forms of Christianity that use a more modern style of worship—music, an emphasis on interaction among individuals, and a personal relationship with God.

What we are seeing more of now, and what I like, and what can exist in both Catholicism and Protestantism, is an emphasis on a personal relationship with God and a sincerity of belief that has not been vocally expressed by many congregations before, though this kind of sincerity has been clear in the black church for a long time.

People will most often call people who practice this kind of Christianity "born-again" Christians, and use "born-again" to mean "conservative" or "fanatical" when all it really means is someone who has made an earnest decision to become a Christian. I worry that the word "Christian" is being hijacked to mean "conservative" when really what it means is "follower of Christ," who was in his day a real radical and always trying to improve the lives of all men.

To me, it's a style of worship. In traditional churches, you sing hymns and praise God. You're singing the words, but there's no driving force. Modern churches tend to have a lot more young people; it's a lot more exciting. It's more of a celebration. There's something about a guitar and drums—it just gets you going in a different way. There's a lot more emphasis on fellowship, small-group stuff, and people talking to each other about their beliefs.

Throughout this whole thing, I was questioning a lot of stuff. It was my first quarter in college, and all this stuff was going on, and I was just totally blown away. There were a lot of moments where I was, "I feel like I'm OK with saying that I believe in Christ." But then I would get really upset about it—like the whole thing made me really, really anxious. Then I was like, "I guess I don't have it, I don't believe, I don't know."

MY FAITH JOURNEY

Rethinking Priorities

I never felt comfortable saying anything out loud. Then eventually, I just did. It was this growing feeling of becoming more and more comfortable with that side of myself. If you're a going-all-the-way type of person like me, things are important to you and you shape your life around them. So deciding you are going to be religious is a big thing because it makes you rethink priorities and makes you rethink how you relate to the world in general.

It was really scary. It was awful. It was almost a horrible experience. I felt like I was giving up my entire identity, especially raised like I was, in this very liberal family. In high school I was very liberal and I was very critical of people who are conservative Christians. I made jokes—there's the whole "Jesus-freak" thing. In my younger days, I had no problem with that brand of humor. But to be totally on the flip side of that, and all of a sudden to be on the defensive when people make comments—it's a totally bizarre experience.

I think college has also been great for me in that it exposes you to so many different people. I didn't know any conservatives growing up. So I never really heard rational arguments for conservative opinions. And then I came to college and I met all these really intelligent, thoughtful people who I like a lot, who have opinions that are on the other side of the spectrum from where I am. It makes everything so much more complicated, and it makes me so much more indecisive.

I have a good friend. He's Christian and he's pretty conservative. He's one of the most intelligent people I know. He's pro–death penalty, pro-life, pro–this war [Iraq]. But we both respect each other a lot. Our common bond, or the thing that makes us good friends, is our faith and a way of looking at the world, which is exactly the same despite the fact that we disagree about everything.

At college I've definitely met a lot more people who are modern Christians who have an active faith. And being able to talk with people about that has been an amazing thing. Again, it's a type of sincerity that I never knew growing up. Being able to see that and inch my way toward being more like that has been a very cool experience.

My mom has been supportive. She'll never stop being a Catholic. She thinks it's really important. I don't understand a lot of it, but I can definitely respect that commitment. My dad has been critical, but he raised us to make our own decisions. But you can tell when your parents are frustrated by a situation or don't necessarily approve of what's going on.

I tend to think that we're all driving at the same thing and that we're all talking about the same issues, but in a different way. Do I think Christ is the Savior? Yes, I believe in that. But I don't believe that you must believe in Christ to be saved. Whenever I get in this conversation with people who do believe that Christ is the "only way," I usually lose the Biblical-text part of the debate. But I tend to think that if you're driving toward the truth, God will understand that. And if you're trying to live a good life, then you're rewarded for that.

To me, it's not a message of judgment, but one of love, in which we put the needs of others, of society, ahead of our own. It makes me see success not as how much I achieve in life—how much money I make, how much prestige I gain—but as how many lives I can improve. And by improving the lives of others I improve my own. I become a better person.

Something that's been really true for me is that you can't force yourself to be ready to believe and you can't force other people to be ready to believe. It's just something that happens when it happens. There is a reason why I stopped going to church when I was sixteen—it helped me get to the point that I am at now. I needed that separation time to figure things out. So I have a tremendous amount of respect for people who don't go to church, especially when they have a reason for not going to church, because I did that.

People have to be really patient, not only with others, but with themselves. You're never supposed to reach a point where you're like, "I know the absolute truth." The point is to be thinking about it all the time. If you think about it all the time, you're going to come up with new questions all the time, and you're going to doubt things all the time. But that's the way it's supposed to be.

I think a spiritual life is really, really important. That doesn't mean you should start with the church. It just means that you should start thinking about issues, and I think that constant contemplation is going to lead you in the right direction.

A lot of it is talking to people honestly about faith. You just have to make sure you're conveying the fact that you're genuinely interested and you're not being critical, because it is an extremely personal thing to tell people about. People who are religious want to tell people their story. It's funny, because I feel pretty spiritually stable at the moment. This is probably the most stable I've felt my entire life, and at the same time, I know that there's going to be stuff ahead that's going to throw me for a loop and make me doubt and

MY FAITH JOURNEY

question things. I'm twenty years old, and I'm humble enough to know that you can never know anything for sure.

Do I think and do I hope I'm going to have this belief for the rest of my life? Yeah, because it's an amazing thing. At the same time, I'm sure that there are going to be periods of really intense doubt and questioning and stuff that I'm going to go through that's going to make me rethink everything. But hopefully I'll always hold onto this. I intend to at the moment, anyway.

Breaking the Law

How can you be a good person? And beyond that, how can you be a good Christian, Muslim, or Jew?

The answers to these questions fill volumes of holy books. Each religion provides followers with rules or laws to live by. Having to observe these rules and resist the temptation to break them is something that most of the people I interviewed have struggled with.

As they stepped further out into the world and responsibility for their behavior shifted from their parents to themselves, many reexamined their notions of good and bad while navigating an obstacle course of temptations. The temptations are fueled by advertisements that glorify materialism and sex, music videos that promote violence and vanity, and television shows that exalt cheating and greed. With a click of a mouse, pornography can be downloaded from the Internet and gossip can be disseminated to millions of people.

How do young people deal with the clashing contradictions between the ideals promoted in their churches, synagogues, and mosques and the values sold by a market-driven youth culture?

We're Just Born Naturally
Wanting to Do What's Wrong

Julie,* 20
Christian (nondenominational)
*not her real name

We're all born without the desire to do good. And you don't desire to do good until you become a Christian. Being a Christian has been such a blessing because it helps me decide what's good and what's bad, and it helps me in the way I treat other people.

And being a Christian has helped me to remain pure until I get married, if I ever get married. Most people these days do not save sex for marriage. Christians believe that premarital sex is wrong.

We're just born naturally wanting to do what's wrong. And the world doesn't see it as wrong. If you go out and interview a bunch of people, they will say there is nothing wrong with pornography, for instance. And yet the Bible tells us very clearly not to think impure thoughts and to look upon what is lovely.

I like the book of 1 Corinthians because it's so encouraging. There's one verse in there that touches me. It comes from 1 Corinthians 10:13: "No temptation has seized you except what is common to man. And God is faithful; he will not let you be tempted beyond what you can bear. But when you are tempted, he will also provide a way out so that you can stand up under it."

See, the Father is not a standoffish God. He is right there with us. It reminds me that Jesus walked this earth and he was tempted and he overcame it. And he's there to help us overcome it. It's comforting; it's encouraging.

I think it's [U.S. Attorney General] John Ashcroft who said that the difference between the Muslim faith and the Christian faith is that the Christian God sent his son to die for the world and the Muslim God sent Muslim people to die for their own sins. The Christian God is an unselfish God. The Muslim God is a God who demands from his people—he doesn't just say, "Here's a free gift, accept it and you shall live." He says, "You have to work your way."

And none of us can work our way, because like the Bible says, "Not by works lest any man should boast." It means that even with all of our good intentions, unless we're purified by the blood of Jesus Christ, we still can't get into heaven, because justice demands that someone pay for the sin that we do commit.

God created us perfect in the beginning. And then Adam and Eve did what he said not to—they ate the fruit. And we're all paying for it. I don't think that God necessarily thinks that we're awful, horrible people. He loves us. It's just that he's a just God. Justice demands payment.

God is so merciful and good, he sent his son to bear the burden of everything that we do wrong, because he loves us. "For God so loved the world that he gave his only begotten son, that whosoever believes in Him might not perish but have everlasting life." That's from John 3:16. **When we become saved, we are no longer slaves to sin—we are slaves to righteousness.** We have no power before that transformation to say no to a carnal pleasure but afterwards, by the grace of God, we can.

I've Broken Many Commandments

Jack, 14
Interfaith Family (Jewish and Christian)

The first book of Genesis is about Adam and Eve. We discussed it in English class. We read the first two passages of Genesis and talked about temptation. I guess that kind of struck me. We are faced with temptations every day, and the question is: how do we deal with them?

I've broken many commandments—not like "do not kill" or "do not commit adultery." But I've worshipped false idols. I used to idolize Michael Jordan when I was a little kid. I used to be a gigantic fan of the Bulls when they were good. I've broken a lot of the 613 commandments[13]—like you can't eat standing up. I've broken kosher.

There are some aspects of the Bible that I don't believe actually happened. There are some aspects that I think are true, but I think they're just metaphors for something that we have to look harder at.

There were people who had their heads chopped off for no good reason. The only people I can think of, besides Jesus, who were actually good people were the odd ones out, like the taxman and the pious Jew.

---

[13] The Mishneh Torah lists 613 *mitzvot* or commandments.

There are just some horrible people in the Bible. I don't know if I like them. But then, that's what makes it interesting. You don't read a book if every single person in the book is good. There's got to be a bad guy and there's got to be a good guy.

The only one I can think of who was pure goodness was Jesus. I admire Jesus. I wouldn't put a fish on the back of my car, but I think he's the least corrupted of all the people in the Bible. That's because he's the Son of God.

But I don't think he's the Son of God. I think he's an image of God, someone that we should live by. God is not a person. God is a guideline. God is saying, "Live by these rules and you should do fine in life."

Admittance

A poem is a capsule where we wrap our most punishable secrets.

William Carlos Williams

Daniel, 21
Christian (Catholic)

I will never admit that I have wanted to hurt a woman.
I will never admit that I have been attracted to men.

I will never admit that I like that "Heart Goes On" song by Celine Dion.
I will never admit how much the "cool" kids scare me.
I will never admit how I imagined killing bullies.

I will never admit to drinking heavily alone.
I will never admit that I punch walls.
I will never admit I have burned myself with matches just to feel.

I will never admit that I stop watching pornography if the girl is
    wearing a cross.
I will never admit that I change the station when a lyric is
    semi-sacrilegious.
I will never admit how scared I am that I might not believe in God.

I will never admit that I really enjoy cleavage.
I will never admit how I have fallen in love with any girl
    that has shown interest.
I will never admit to the numbness when she walks away.
I will never admit how close I was to putting this poem's first
    two lines here instead.

Daniel is a graduate of Young Chicago Authors, an arts education program for Chicago youth.

Temptation Is in Every Corner

Hesed, 14
Christian (United Methodist)

Some people say that if you're trying to convert people to Christianity, don't tell them about hell because that will scare them. But that's misleading people, because hell is a very big part of Christianity. People have always feared it. You can't leave out the part that being a Christian isn't easy.

Jesus said, "If you want to be my disciple, you've got to take up your cross and follow me every day." **And being a teenager in a very atheistic society, it's almost like going through mockery every day—just stereotyping and being cast out.** I've had best friends leave me partly because of being a Christian. You'll get ridiculed. Just being a high schooler and having all the pressures and all the cliques and expectations—I think that that's the hardest.

High school is the place where you want to belong. Basically, if you're not accepted in high school, life can be very, very, very miserable. Junior high and high school are where you're trying to figure out who you are—and most of the time, at least somewhere along the way—you conform, because this is what's cool and this is what's accepted. Nobody wants to feel left out, and no one wants to be the geek or the freak walking down the hall who has no friends.

For girls, there are the tight jeans and lowriders. Being a girl, I know I want to wear those jeans. I'll wear them, but it depends on who I'm with. If you're going to be with guys, if you're smart, you won't wear them. You don't want to cause other people to stumble because of what you wear.

Dating

Dating is a big thing. I know a lot of friends who do it [have sex]. A lot of people have done it since sixth grade, seventh grade, and all through junior high. I have a True Love Waits ring. It's a purity ring. I wear it and my guy friends know where I stand—it's like, "No, I'm sorry." There's the practical side to it, like I want to be a doctor, and having a baby really won't get me there at all. But there are also moral issues with what the Bible says about sexual purity.

Wait is what I'm going to do. But along the way it's like I'm living out my principles in a surrounding where temptation is in every corner. Just like in terms of, how far will you go in a relationship? How far do you go in dating in general? What's acceptable and what's not? And clothing, and just moral issues in a world where a lot of things are immoral. I think that's really the big temptation—to conform and do things you don't think are right.

Hesed describes the halls of a junior high school where temptation seems to be all around. Not surprisingly, holding onto religious ideals in those surroundings is tough.

Sometimes I Snap

Front row: Tanisha, 16; Arianna, 17; Laura, 16; Domonique, 17
Back row: Martin, 17; Christina; 17; Yvette, 17; James,14

Laura: When I'm around people and they listen to secular songs and do different dances, I want to fit in. You conform to your friends. So I'll do the dances too. When I started doing that, I lost myself, I lost where I came from. R. Kelly, B2K, Missy Elliott, and artists of that sort—they promote sex and materialistic things. I've got to stop myself and say, "This is not you. You're supposed to be living a life for God."

Martin: I'm starting to figure out that I'm not strong enough in my faith yet to where I can sit down and I can listen to secular music and I can flush it out. It sticks. It's something that God has just revealed to me. He's slowly but surely showing me that, "You still a baby. You're trying to run, but you can barely crawl."

Domonique: I listen to secular music. Some of it is uplifting, like Mariah Carey's "Through the Rain." It's not exactly a Christian song, but it's not downgrading women, or telling you, "Let's go buy this" or "Let's go have sex." But some secular music has a lot of sexual implications in it and steers us away from our focus on God. There are some songs that I'm strong enough to handle and listen to—I'll just let them go through one ear and out the other. I will let those singles play. But if it's something that I know I'm not old enough to listen to, not strong enough to listen to, then I'll turn from it.

Arianna: Like Domonique said—she knows her limits and will not listen to certain things that she knows she can't handle. I don't think I'm necessarily there. Like sometimes when I'm listening to something, I get that feeling and I want to turn, but then I don't turn. And it's like, "Ooo, I know that was bad." I kind of zone it out, and then I don't zone it out. If you're constantly listening to certain things, it can get into your spirit. You start moving yourself the wrong way. And then you start wearing clothes that are more revealing because you think that you'd like to look like this certain celebrity.

Christina: My family is not really into church. So if I'm in the car with my mama and I turn to a gospel station, she's like, "Uh-uh. I don't want to hear that." And all my friends play secular music. When I'm riding in the car with them I'm trying to tune it out. I think there's a struggle within me. I hear this song, and I'm like, "Ooo, this got a nice beat. I'm not going to turn to WCGI 1390—they be playin' some old crazy songs, some old-time religion songs."

Martin: I believe the reason why we are so passionate toward certain things is because that's a desire of our heart that the Lord has given to us. You can't just up and say one day, "I'm not going to listen to secular music anymore." That's like a cigarette smoker trying to give up smoking cold turkey—nine times out of ten, it doesn't work. You're not going to throw all of your CDs away, and you're not going to change your station to gospel radio, or whatever. There's a process and there's prayer that goes into it. You pray to God and do the things that he tells you. If everything was a snap—if you could give up everything that causes you to sin in your life—everybody would be perfect.

Christina: People don't give you a hard time about listening to Christian music. But they give you a hard time when you say you're Christian. You have to really be walking a straight line in order to tell somebody what they can do and what they cannot do. If I am singing an R&B song—it doesn't even have to be a bad song; like I could be singing Mariah Carey, she's not a gospel artist. They're like, "Why are you singing her song?" They watch everything you do, and they criticize everything you say. They expect you to be perfect.

James: Another thing is gossiping. I try to separate myself from that. Some people might tell me something, and I'm like, "OK, that's nice," and I don't say anything about it. But sometimes . . .

Tanisha: My biggest problem is talking about people—it became a habit. If your gown is lime green and you've got on yellow shoes, I'm just going to say something about it. But it shouldn't matter what you have on. You should love your neighbor in spite of everything. You shouldn't be saying anything negative about somebody.

Christina: Everybody has to say something about everybody, and it becomes a habit. It's hard to break that habit. The reason it's a sin is because God made everybody in his image. And if you're talking about somebody, you're basically saying that God didn't make that person right. Who are you to say that God made a mistake?

Domonique: The thing that is a real struggle is profanity. My freshman and sophomore years, every other sentence I would curse. But now I've learned how to control my speaking, and so I don't curse like I used to. But I have a temper problem, so if I get really mad and I snap, it just rolls off my tongue.

Since last year I've been trying to work on what comes out of my mouth. I've learned how to calm down, and when people are cussing me out, I'm just like, "Jesus loves you, too. If it boosts your self-esteem to talk about me, then you go right ahead. I'm all for helping people." But sometimes I snap and I can't help it.

There's Always That One Person That Pushes Your Buttons

Wesley, 16
Christian (Catholic)

You've always got to be the nice guy, and sometimes you just don't want to be the nice guy. There's always that one person that pushes your buttons. And you're always supposed to treat them like they're your neighbors. The Bible says you gotta do it, so you gotta do it. It's all in the Ten Commandments, and it basically states, "Treat everybody like you want to be treated." I don't want someone pushing my buttons, so I'm not going to push his. And hopefully he'll respond right.

You have your sensitive subjects. And some people just want to take that and use that against you. They keep poking fun at that one thing that really, really bothers you. And you tell them, "I don't want to talk about that." And then they keep going and going. And you just want to flip out at them, and you're not supposed to.

Like last year this guy kept picking on me. He was trying to joke around. He said, "You're just a stupid jock, you're a meathead." And I was like, "I'm not a meathead, and I don't want to be called a meathead. I try as hard as I can in school." And he kept picking on me until I just said, "That's enough, I don't want to talk to you anymore." I turned my back and walked away. And he jumped on my back and put me in a headlock and slammed my face against the floor.

I just sat there, and I said, "I'm not going to do anything." He got off and walked away before the school cops came in. I had a bloody lip. I didn't want to fight back.

I think fighting is just stupid. When this whole war in Iraq came about, I was one of what the public calls "those idiots on TV" that were protesting. I did a silent protest at school. We wore armbands that said "No war in Iraq," and we didn't talk for the day. We got funny looks, and people actually said, "You know, you're weird."

I think my religious belief in the whole "treat everyone like your brother" has led me to be a pacifist. I think it's a great thing. If you can solve everything nonviolently, without any sort of pain, that includes mental pain, I think that's the way.

For many religiously observant Americans, faith is more than something you do one day a week when you go to worship services. It's a way of life. Religious teachings dictate even the smallest details of their lives.

For many of the Muslims I spoke with, the greatest challenge to following their faith was finding the time and the place to pray.

"You Get Up and You Pray!"

Sarah, 21
Muslim

My religion is an active religion. You pray five times a day. When I was living at home in high school, if it was time for a prayer and I didn't get up, my mom would be like, "You get up and you pray!" I would see my parents and my brother and sister, and that would remind me.

My first year in college, my roommate was also a Pakistani Muslim girl. When we both started out, we were on task. I got real involved with the mosque on campus, and then school would get busy or some friends would say, "Let's go out." It's almost like you get lazy—it's not always in front of you. I wasn't praying every day as much as I should have.

There have been times when I didn't feel that I was religious at all and it didn't bug me at all. Then two weeks, three weeks, four weeks later, I'd be like, "Wow, I haven't prayed in a week. What's wrong with me?"

I think it was more of a growing-up kind of thing, too. My parents weren't there, they weren't watching, I didn't have to. But as I got older—twenty, twenty-one—it hit me that I wasn't doing it for my parents anyway. God was still watching.

I had a roommate who was more religious than I was. There's a morning prayer at sunrise, and nowadays that's like 4:58. There's an evening prayer at night before you sleep, after nine or ten o'clock. There were a lot of times when I wouldn't get up for the morning one. I realized that she was, so I started asking her to wake me up when she got up. That helped.

At night I'd be tired. We'd come home from the library at eleven or twelve, study until one or two, and I'd just want to go to sleep. And I'd see her still praying before she slept. She's doing it; I should get up, too. That would motivate me.

I Started Just Praying Wherever I Was

Hasan, 22
Muslim

I was in Sunday school at the Muslim Community Center for about eight years. I didn't like going to Sunday school because I'd miss the Bears games. I remember my mom telling me, "One day, you're going to thank me." I was like, "No way." I didn't realize it until now, but yeah, I'm really glad that I went, because if I didn't have my Muslim friends, I'd probably be a wayward youth. I'd probably be hanging out with the wrong crowd.

In high school I was teetering between being a hard-core Muslim and the passive type. I prayed five times a day. When you're like fourteen, if you didn't pray at your school, you're like, "That's cool, I can always make it up." Sometimes if I was at a movie or something, I'd be like, "It's time to pray—I'll do it when I get home."

But if I was with my cousins, these girls would get up and start praying somewhere, and I'd feel like such a loser. I'd be like, they're praying and I'm a man—I have to do something. So I started just praying wherever I was. I'd go to a hockey game, and when it was time to pray, we'd go to a corner and pray. As you mature and you take your religion more seriously, you're like, "I don't care what these people say. I have to pray. It's just my right." You have to stand up for what you believe in.

I was involved in the Muslim Student Association in high school. MSA has kept me grounded. We had our MSA meetings at the end of the day. We had this room, and we'd stay after and pray and talk about things. That was a time when people didn't pray much in their schools, it was really unheard of. They always saw us as extremists just because we prayed.

If we were talking about adultery in class and I said it's a sin in our religion, someone would say, "God, is that all you're about?" People think that our religion restricts us so much. It's just that our religion and American society are so counter to each other. But the fact is that our religion does not condone some things. We can't rationalize and say, "We're in America, we can drink because everyone around us drinks." Just because our religion is different doesn't mean that we're some alien-type people.

When I left high school, I said MSA is the place for me. That is where I won't lose my way—I'll always be kept in check.

When I came to the University of Illinois, the MSA had a room on the eighth floor. We used to pray together up there. Then they had to remodel that area. Now it's difficult. You have to pray in an isolated corner. It's noisy. People are walking around. You really can't concentrate. Concentration is really key in prayer—it's just you and God. But people are walking around and looking at you. They make you feel like you're some object of scorn and scrutiny.

We have a couple of rooms reserved for Friday prayer, *Jumma*. Friday prayers are very important for men. It's twenty-seven times better to pray with someone else than to pray alone. I think that's what the function of the MSA is—to establish a Friday prayer. And if that's established, you can count yourself as successful because you've made a place for people to pray. They have to obey God, and you're helping them do that.

When I spoke with observant Jews about the practice of their faith, they often spoke of halachah, or Jewish law. On the following pages, Jews explain some of the basic tenets of Jewish law and how it both complicates and enriches their lives.

"How Can You Give Up All of This Stuff Because of Your Religion?"

Rebecca, 17
Jewish (Conservative)

In the Bible, in the Torah, there are 613 commandments. They involve everything from how you treat other people, to Jewish holidays and how we observe them, and the Sabbath, which is every week, and how we observe that. It's like a guide how to live.

There are also a lot of dietary laws. The dietary laws say we can only eat certain kinds of meat that are killed and prepared in a certain way. We can't eat meat at nonkosher restaurants. My parents like to remind me of this funny story. One time when I was two, we were driving past a Burger King. I saw the sign, and I yelled out, "That sign says Burger King. No burgers for Jewish people." I picked up on those observances. It was always something that was a part of me. I recognized that it was important.

We set the Sabbath aside as a day of rest because God rested on the seventh day after creating the world. Because of this, there are lots of rules for things you can and can't do. I started to observe them more strictly after my bat mitzvah. It's supposed to be a day of rest—you're not supposed to do any type of work, or watch television, use the computer, use electricity, any of that stuff.

When I was younger I used to think that if I stayed home all day, and watched TV, and got on my computer—that would be resting. Then I decided to try observing it more strictly to see how it felt. For me it's very spiritual. It really separates the day out from the rest of the week.

I spend a lot of time with my family—from Friday night at sundown until Saturday night. I go to prayers at my synagogue in the morning and sometimes in the afternoon. It's just a really spiritual experience. It makes it more of an important day. You can't cook. You can't spend money, either. We eat food that was prepared before or we eat cold food.

I haven't gone to see a movie on a Saturday or Friday night ever.

It's weird being in a public high school because you're faced with being in a school where there's a lot of activities on Friday nights and things to miss out on. Like all the school plays are on Friday nights. I have to give up trying out for school plays. And sports—I used to play softball. But there are games every Saturday, so I couldn't play in those.

A lot of people look at it like, "How can you give up all of this stuff because of your religion?" It's just a matter of how you look at it. You can look at it as being a burden—that you have all these religious obligations, so you're not able to do your school activities. But I look at it as a more positive experience. It's something that I choose to do.

One thing that is fulfilling is the sense of community that religion provides. One of the things that initially attracted me to it is having a group that you feel close with, which is what I have with my synagogue community and also in my youth-group community. It's a sense of belonging, like you're here for a reason.

It's easy to get caught up in everyday life. And everything that goes on in our world is so focused on success, making money. Judaism helps you step back from that—look at what's really important, our values, family and friends, the way we treat other people, the way we treat ourselves, what we're here for.

"Will You Let Me Take Sabbath Off?"

Darcy, 23
Jewish (Modern Orthodox)

If you're an Orthodox Jew, it shapes your life in a way that most people do not realize, in that it also shapes what your career goals are. For example, I wanted to be an event planner. It's something I'm very good at. But I can't in this country because most events are held on Saturday or Friday nights, and if you're the planner you have to be there to supervise and make sure everything goes off smoothly. That's something I'm automatically barred from doing, unless I do only Jewish religious events.

It's hard because every time I look for a job, I can't do anything that would make me break a law, so I have to make sure, "Will you let me take Sabbath off? Will I have to travel over the weekend?" because I can't do this job if I have to travel then. "Will you be flexible in terms of giving me random days off during the year for Jewish holidays?" The dates of the holidays change in the secular calendar.

I can't do any food tasting—wine tasting, restaurant critic—since that would make me violate the dietary laws, and there isn't enough demand for a food critic who only does kosher restaurants. If you're not an observant Jew, you don't realize how much that changes what you can and can't do, and in so doing, shapes your career.

One thing that drives all Orthodox Jews crazy is when we are trying to explain to non-Jews why we cannot do something—like come in to work on Saturday—and they reply, "That's not true. I have a Jewish friend, and they come to work on Saturday." Then they are convinced that we are trying to lie to them and cheat them, since what we are saying is obviously a false excuse, and we can't just say, "Yes, well, your friend isn't religious!"

Many religions impose dietary restrictions on followers because of concerns about health and animal cruelty. Also, restrictions on diet, including fasting, teach people self-control, appreciation for what they have, and empathy for the less fortunate.

Many Christians fast and avoid restricted foods during Lent. Observant Jews strive to keep kosher or follow Jewish dietary laws. And Muslims abide by Islamic teachings on what and what not to eat and drink.

Jewish dietary laws are derived from text in the Hebrew Bible. The very basic rules are 1) don't eat certain kinds of meat—including pork and shellfish, and 2) don't mix dairy and meat. Orthodox rabbis make the final decision about whether or not certain foods, manufacturers, and eating establishments can be certified as kosher.

Muslim dietary laws also forbid Muslims from eating pork and pork products. To be halal, *the Muslim equivalent of kosher, animals must be slaughtered a particular way. Alcohol is also prohibited.*

There are a number of kosher bakeries, butcher shops, restaurants, and grocery stores in areas with large Jewish populations. And the number of halal food outlets is growing. Yet observant Muslims and Jews say that mealtimes often present challenges.

I Really Wanted a Hot Dog

Adina, 16
Jewish (Conservative)

I keep kosher. But I don't do it as strictly as some people. Some people wait six hours from meat to milk—I wait two, sometimes less. Some people won't eat in a restaurant if it's not strictly CRC-approved kosher.[14]

Today I was at our youth-group event, and I really wanted a hot dog, and it was a company I knew was kosher. So then I had to ask about their bread—"Can I see the label on the bread to make sure there's no dairy in it?" And there wasn't. So I got a hot dog from a hot-dog stand, which is something I normally would not do.

I only eat at certain restaurants. I hang out with a very religious group of kids so they understand. We're all different religions, but they all understand that I need to be doing this. You're brought up with the same traditions and the same values, regardless of whether or not it's the same religion. Like what things define a good person or a bad person? All these things are so parallel in all the religions, yet we seem to not be able to get along. It boggles my mind.

One of my friends was raised Jewish but doesn't believe it so much anymore. That's who you get more grief from. She'll bring pork for lunch and say, "Umm, it's so-o-o good! Yum, yum, yum." She'll just shove it in my face.

Many of the people I talked to described their level of religious observance as something that rose and fell. They were more religious at certain times in their lives and less religious at others. One of these people is Dan. He describes his struggle to become more observant, how keeping kosher and observing Jewish law is a part of this struggle, and why this is important to him.

---

[14] CRC stands for Chicago Rabbinical Council.

You're Striving to Be a Better Jew

Dan, 20
Jewish

My journey in Judaism, so to speak, is something that's just been ongoing. My level of observance is up and down. But I feel that it doesn't matter. It's not the level of Judaism that you're at, but that you're constantly striving to take on more—you're striving to be a better Jew. I always try to keep my observance going up rather than going down.

My father grew up in an observant household. He'd gone through a yeshiva and he'd done quite a bit of learning when he was young.[15] My mother, on the other hand, grew up in an Israeli secular house. There are a fair amount of religious Jews in Israel, but most Israelis are secular Jews.

My mom is a secular Jew. She prefers to take the beautiful aspects of Judaism—the traditions, the art, the customs, and stuff like that—as opposed to Jewish law, which to her and many people seems antiquated. My mom was never fully observant, and my father gave up being fully observant.

We'd always have dinner on Friday nights, ritual dinners. My mom cooked big meals for the holidays. I learned how to read and write Hebrew. When I was younger, my father and I would go to the synagogue every Saturday. My house was definitely more observant than the typical American Jewish household, but it wasn't observant by what one would consider an Orthodox standard.

Over time, I've increased my stringency, and I've started to take on a higher level of observance. I used to keep just basic kosher—not eating meat and cheese, not eating pig. And after a while, I would only eat kosher-certified meat. And then I stopped eating cheese that's not kosher-certified.

It gets tricky. You want to go out and eat at these places with your friends. But after a while, you just take it as a given. There are things that I miss—I don't get much pizza. But it's not that bad. I feel that by trying to keep more kosher, by trying to eat more kosher foods, it's an improvement.

I believe that there is a level of spirituality in doing certain things. Aside from just following law, doing these things allows me to feel more connected to the religion. It allows me to pay respect to the laws. It adds a good feeling.

---

[15] A yeshiva is a religious school.

My father said, "Do what you're comfortable with. Don't push yourself too much. Don't restrict yourself." Sometimes my mom is like, "Why would you not travel on Sabbath? Why would you restrict yourself? There's no aesthetic value to that." And so we'd bicker about it.

Obviously, I wouldn't be doing these things if I felt that Torah, or the laws, or Judaism itself was just a bunch of crock. It's part of my decision to try to follow halachah, Jewish law, more stringently. I've had to take on more things, and it doesn't bother me so much. It's tough, but I think that it's rewarding. You should never view it as a burden. The whole point is to do it with joy and happiness.

I think that's the thing with faith—you're going to be tested. I think the tough situations are designed to make us stronger so that when tougher situations come out, we can deal with them better.

Faith can help you deal with the future. It's very important to have this hope for the future that's instilled through faith; otherwise, how are you going to go on? You know that something will come in the future, that there will be some sort of resolution—that things will get better.

Sexual promiscuity and sex outside of marriage are taboo in many religious teachings. Yet most religious Americans live by a different set of rules regarding sexual behavior. By their late teens, an estimated three out of four Americans have had sexual intercourse, according to the Alan Guttmacher Institute. Sex infuses every part of popular culture from reality TV shows and music videos to teen magazines and the Internet.

How do people deal with religious restrictions on their sexual behavior? This was one of the most difficult challenges, especially for some of the guys I spoke with.

Oh, Hell, I'm At a Strip Club!

Daniel, 21
Christian (Catholic)

My friends and I have a typical group. We have one really good-looking guy who always gets women. I'm the moderately good-looking funny guy who cracks jokes. We have one guy who is just bitter as all hell, and one guy who is kind of crazy. And we go to bars. I'm considered the religious one. I still go to church every Sunday.

I'm twenty-one, and I'm trying to balance what is a fun lifestyle and what everybody else considers a fun lifestyle. You're twenty-one, you know. Your hormones are going crazy—you're finally getting into bars.

We were at a strip club two days ago, and it's like, "Oh, hell, I'm at a strip club!" And it's like, "OK, two days earlier I'm at church, praying the Hail Mary, Our Father, and now I have this stripper sitting next to me." There's a conflict there—like what's respectful to religion, and what do I need to do as a twenty-one-year-old guy?

I think sex and religion—you just kind of separate them. It's nice to have that idea, there's one girl and you marry her and it's fantastic forever. But at the same time, how do you know you're meeting that one girl if you don't go out and meet other girls, and go on dates, and try different things with people? What if I'm in love with this girl, and I meet another girl two days later that I fall in love with?

It's tough. I'm cautious. I have plenty of cousins with kids before twenty. But sometimes, you have to make mistakes.

You're Human, You Like Girls

Ed,* 21
Muslim
*not his real name

I had Muslim friends. I had non-Muslim friends. But the friends I could really identify with were the Muslim ones. Those guys didn't party. I didn't party. We didn't date, drink, smoke, do drugs, or things like that.

Other people made it tough. They poked fun at us. They'd say, "That girl likes you. Why don't you ask her out?" I'd say that I can't. They'd say I was gay or something because I didn't date.

This whole dating thing is toughest for me. You're human, you like girls. Once I was thinking about going to a club. I was talking to one of my cousins, and she said, "What if you die there? You would be dying in a forbidden place." It scared me because Islam is your way of life, and if you're following your religion, you're not at a club or a bar. We don't know when we're going to die, but I wouldn't want to jeopardize the hereafter on some stupid mistake.

I had a non-Muslim friend. He was screwing around, and he'd drag me into it. We went to clubs once or twice. I'd be talking to girls, exchanging numbers, and I'd say to myself, "This is so stupid. What am I doing? I can't live my life like this."

I started dating this one girl. She liked me. I remember we would meet at Barnes & Noble, and I couldn't wait to see her. That was a big mistake. It totally ruined my studying. She was Catholic. She said she was thinking about converting to Islam. She had dated a Pakistani guy before. She said, "He said that if I converted, marriage would be OK." He must have been lying to her. It's very rare for a Caucasian to come into a Pakistani family. I wasn't even thinking about marriage.

I stopped seeing her. Now I have to focus on studying. But there are lots of girls in my classes.

I'm Kind of "Dating God"

Ilene, 18
Christian (born again)

I've never dated in my life. I feel like if I want to date you, I'd be willing to consider you as a potential marriage partner. I just haven't found that person yet. And right now, I'm kind of "dating God." He is who I want to spend my time with and become more like.

I wear a promise ring on my finger where I'll have my wedding ring. My mom gave it to me. I wear it on my finger to remind me of my promise to God and my commitment to stay pure and not have sex until I'm married.

I don't want to put myself in that situation yet. I'm not ready to get married. I totally want a career after I go to college. I would feel it's unfair for the guy because I'm very interested in finishing college and pursuing a career.

This past year, it was weird for me to be on my own. I think this was a time when God was trying to strengthen me. My roommate went on so many dates. And I couldn't help but imagine, whoa, that would be kind of cool, kind of fun. But I knew in my heart that I wasn't ready for that. I have friends who have very healthy dating relationships, and I'm very happy for them. I'm not ready for that.

I have some friends who promised not to kiss until they're married. They promised that they'll just hold hands and not do anything else. A big part of it is just committing your relationship to God and not putting yourself in a situation where you might be by yourself with someone.

I think it's OK to be friends with guys. A big part of it is to have self-control and to trust God and to read his Word so that I could stay strong. When I make decisions, it's just a matter of always going back to the Bible. You should always go back to the Bible and just focus on him always, never compromise, stay strong, continue to read his Word daily.

I Try Every Day to Fight the Jihad of Personal Struggle

Growing up in the U.S., a Muslim girl says she encountered the same pressures and temptations faced by other teenagers. So praying five times a day and being an observant Muslim was challenging. She discovers that spirituality is more than ritual worship.

Maham, 19
Muslim (Ahmadi)

When I walk down the street, people do not identify me as Muslim. People think I'm Italian. If they are experienced, they'll assume I'm from somewhere in the Middle East. Also, I'm so outgoing, and I don't wear the hijab. People hear the word "Muslim" and they assume it's someone who's wearing the hijab, or someone who is really introverted—it's very stereotypical.

My parents are both from Pakistan. My dad was a major in the army there. I was born there, but I was less than a year old when we moved here, so I'm an American citizen. Most Muslims are Sunni. We belong to a new wave of Muslims called the Ahmadiyya Movement. We believe that the Messiah, who everyone is waiting for, has already arrived.

Some of the very radical Muslims in Pakistan are not accepting. My dad dealt with a lot of harassment and prejudice for being an Ahmadi. There was a lot of persecution going on there, a lot of persecution. So my dad decided he was going to leave and come here and start a new life.

We struggled to survive. My dad drove cabs and worked for Whirlpool. He got his degree in marketing. He worked his way up, and now he owns his own contracting company. He's definitely come a very long way. I admire him, truly.

I grew up in Chicago. I've had friends of all sorts, of all cultures and all religions. I have good Christian friends, good Jewish friends, friends who have no religion at all. **Before I'm Muslim, before I'm anything, I'm just a teenager.**

MY FAITH JOURNEY

I'm a kid growing up in America. I'm going to deal with the same pressures.

Did I always go out and buy the most expensive shoes to fit in and be cool? Yes, I did. Anywhere you go, teenagers will always worry about the way they look. I have a friend in Saudi Arabia, and she told me the competition there is who wears their scarf the most elegant way and who has the most expensive scarves. It just shows you that competition is everywhere. It's part of our nature to do that.

I was a very good girl. I used to pray five times a day when I was younger—twelve to fifteen I wouldn't party. I wouldn't touch alcohol. I wasn't forced to avoid it, I was just happy that way. But I was tempted as a teenager, so I had a cigarette once or twice, just "to look cool." And I would try to stay out late after my parents told me not to. (I hope my parents don't read this.) I just wanted to be a teenager.

When I was fifteen, I was really super-religious actually. Then I fell into this not-so-religious stage—that was between the end of junior year of high school and freshman year of college. I started praying less and hanging out with my friends more. I believe that spirituality is a roller coaster and that you're going to have your ups and downs, because when you're up, there's nowhere to go but down. That's how life is.

I went down, and now I think I'm heading right back up. I still am not back to praying five times a day because of my schedule (I try to pray as much as I can), but I believe that true spirituality transcends ritual worship, so I try to live my life with the philosophy that Islam teaches—of compassion, peace, submission, tolerance, and things like that. I try every day to fight the jihad of personal struggle to become a better person.

That's what Islam is to me now, more than just praying five times a day. When you're fourteen, that's enough. But as you mature, life becomes complicated and harder to categorize as just good and bad. The rules are not laid out in black and white anymore—you a find a lot of gray area since you gain more independence as you get older. After all, you start to make your own decisions—some good, some bad—but life has to teach you its lessons somehow.

I do believe in the rituals. Like Ramadan is coming up next week. Do I plan on fasting all thirty days? Yes, I do. Those things help me become a better Muslim. There are a lot of things that are taught in Islam, like wearing the headscarf and praying. Just as people eat food four or five times a day to nourish their bodies, prayers nourish the soul four or five times a day. It's a way for me to meditate. It's a way for me to tune myself out from the things around me that are bad influences. It's a way to remind myself of who I am so I have less chances of doing something I'll regret.

Dating nowadays is all about going out and meeting people, and most of the time, having premarital sex. That's a big no-no in Islam. Dating is prohibited in Islam because it causes a lot of social ills. If people only slept with their spouses, there would be less social ills—less STDs, less illegitimate children.

Is it tempting to date people? Of course it is. I'm not going to lie. I'm nineteen years old and I go to a school where there are good-looking people. You reach a point when you want somebody in your life. So, am I tempted? Yes. If anyone says that they're not, they're lying to you, they're not human.

Arranged Marriage

At work, people will ask, "How do you get married if you're not allowed to date?" I do believe I will find that person. A lot of people think, "Oh, arranged marriages! Oh, my God, how can you do that?" Culture plays a big part of it. There are people who get married to people they have met for the first time, or never met before.[16]

I believe that I will have an arranged marriage—not in the sense that my parents are going to choose someone for me, but rather that God has arranged for someone to be my partner in life. If I continue to strive on the right path, as God has defined it in terms of chastity and purity, then I will deserve to find my soul mate, and surely God will bless me with him.

The only way really to be happy with the concept of arranged marriage is by having infinite and total trust and faith in God. Who knows better than him what is best for me? And I do think that for me, the right person is someone who is the same religion as me. So chances are, I will find that person through exposure to my own community.

That's where my parents come in. They are unbiased facilitators who want the best for their daughter. So I trust them to introduce me to prospects that they know could be a suitable and compatible match. The parents go through a referral system if there are bachelors in the community. It's like a blind date.

---

[16] Although some Muslim-Americans do have arranged marriages, many do not.

MY FAITH JOURNEY

You get set up. If you don't like the person, you don't have to deal with them anymore. If you do find a suitable match, then you get "courted" in a sense, usually via e-mail, or phone, or even visits with a third party present. It's whatever you and your family feel comfortable with. The ultimate goal is dating without the naughtiness. The final choice is in my hands.

Last summer my parents introduced me to a guy. Our families went out for dinner and they let us sit together at a separate table so that we could get past the awkwardness of our parents scrutinizing us. It didn't work out. He and I were on two different pages. But we were able to find that out without the whole trauma of dating.

Whenever my friends ask me if I feel left out of the dating scene, or lonely because I don't have a boyfriend or romance in my life, or sad because I have never even had my first kiss, I say to them, "After watching shows like 'Blind Date,' I don't feel left out." Yes, at times I get lonely and it is hard. But then I remind myself that when I do finally get married, for me it will be all the amazing 'firsts' in one great package—my first real butterflies, my first romance, my first love, and that sweet innocence of a first kiss. I don't think there is anything more romantic than that.

Dissing
My Religion

After the terrorist attacks of September 11, 2001, mosques were vandalized, Muslim-Americans were harassed, and some were physically attacked.

Hostility against Muslim-Americans is deep and widespread. The majority of Muslims I talked to had experienced prejudice. Many felt that their community and their faith were under siege.

Other religious groups have suffered discrimination in the U.S. For example, anti-Semitism has dogged Jewish-Americans. A generation ago, anti-Catholic prejudice was acceptable and widespread—some Catholics report that it still exists. And being religious in itself is cause for put-downs and rejection.

On the following pages, you'll read about religious stereotypes and intolerance and how people responded when they encountered them.

We're Supposed to Be Perfect

Domonique, 17
Christian (Protestant)

You've got to be a role model and almost perfect to be around certain people in my school. It's like, "Oh, did you just curse, Miss Christian? No, you didn't! Oh, no, you're not a Christian." It's stuff like that. They hold us to a higher standard and watch everything we do. We're teenagers, so of course we're going to slip up sometimes. We're not perfect.

Or if we just happen to go out one day, they're like, "You're not supposed to go out on dates," "Ooo, you kissed him," things like that. I think they believe that we're supposed to be perfect—that we're supposed to have no flaws at all and that's what a real Christian is. So if we make one slight mistake, they're like, "Oh, you're not a Christian."

If we try to interfere with something—break up a fight or calm down an argument—they say, "Miss Goody Two Shoes" or "Miss Christian Lady." They think that we try to hold ourselves above them because we're Christians.

"You're One of *Those* Guys?"

Daniel, 21
Christian (Catholic)

In the world today, religion is such a roll-your-eyes type thing. I tell people that I go to church every Sunday, and they're, "Oh, really? You're one of those guys?"

I'm not. I go to church every Sunday, and it's a part of me. But I'm still a guy. Here I am. Here is my religion. Don't judge me on it. Don't assume things about me. Don't say, "He goes to church every Sunday, so let's not call him if we want to go out to a bar."

I hate the stigma that is applied to religion—that if you're religious, you're weird. Like you don't like to have fun, and on Saturday nights you just sit at home with a movie. I'd rather be out dancing at a bar having a good time.

If somebody says they don't believe, I don't try to convert them, because there was a period when I didn't believe in it. I don't think it's good to have people tell you what to think. **The only reason my faith is as healthy as it is, is**

because I found it on my own terms. I know lapsed Catholics who worry and feel bad. They still believe in God and Jesus, but they don't go to mass. I'm like, you gotta do what you gotta do. I believe it's such a personal journey that it really does no good for me to be like, "This is my testimony."

Being Christian Does Not Top the Cool List

Hesed, 14
Christian (United Methodist)

Being Christian does not top the cool list at all. For a guy, being a player or an athlete does. If you're a girl, wearing skimpy outfits does. And knowing how to dance, or being a cheerleader, is basically what tops the list. Or being willing to go to parties, drink, smoke, and go to third base. Being a Christian just kind of lowers you down. You're still cool if you have other things going for you, but being a Christian isn't a seeked-out attribute in a person.

Being a pastor's kid, I hear jokes like, "She's so good and holy and pure." And it makes it really hard for me to commit a mistake. I put pressure on myself not to mess up. If I'm saying I'm a Christian, I give people the impression of Christianity by my actions.

I'm not saying I'm perfect at all. If I slam into a table by accident, the S word comes out once in a while. People are like, "She said the S word! She's going to hell!" It's meant as a joke, and I don't take it personally.

All of my friends have stereotypes about church being hymnals and slow organ music that puts you to sleep and long sermons and condemnations. I invite them to our youth group, and they're surprised to hear rock music and fast-paced contemporary worship songs. Worship can be fun.

Catholic and Protestant

I have a lot of friends who don't consider Catholics Christians. I ask them, "Are they Christians?" They're like, "No, they're Catholics." My dad talks to me about it all the time—why Christianity is so divided with all the denominations it has. Basically, I'm Methodist, and in general, I'm Protestant, because there are some doctrines and practices of the Catholic Church that I don't believe are compatible with the Bible.

I've been taught by my dad and other theologians that we're all Christians even if you're Catholic. I think we just have this division in what we believe is right. In Christianity, the great division is that we, United Methodists and other Protestant denominations, believe that you are saved by grace, and that doing good works is a result of grace. And since you're saved by grace, you're going to heaven no matter what, as long as you believe. Catholics believe that you're saved by grace and good works. We disagree with different beliefs in the Catholic faith, but Jesus is still in the middle. If Jesus Christ is the center of your denomination, that's Christianity.

I consider Catholics Christians. I think some of them are misled. I disagree with having to go to a priest to confess your sins. I don't think it's necessary for there to be a liaison between me and God.

I don't believe in praying to saints or that saints are responsible for certain things. Like if you're selling a house, you pray to this saint—I just think that that's making them idols, and the Ten Commandments say, "No other god before me" and that idolatry is not good. That is why I'm Protestant and Reformed Church.

Animosity between Catholics and Protestants is rooted in differences in belief and practice that began in sixteenth-century Europe. That's when Protestants broke away from the Roman Catholic Church in a long, bloody struggle called the Reformation.

The disagreements over belief and practice that drove Catholics and Protestants apart more than 500 years ago still trigger controversy today.

This Is Who I Am

Pablo, 24
Christian (Catholic)

They were opening up a prayer group at my college. I showed up, and one of the leaders asked, "So what's your faith?" I said I'm a Catholic. I shouldn't have said that. She got on my case. She was a Protestant. She was trying to make me understand that I was wrong. She was arguing against the whole veneration of Mary. She said, "Mary is not the mother of God." The rosary usually involves venerating Mary, kind of like saying a prayer to Mary. That's why it's not accepted by the Protestant religion.

The symbolism in the church—the crucifix with the body of Christ hanging on it, communion, the sacraments[17]—that's what this girl had an issue about.

I've been attacked several times by Protestants. Some Protestants attack the fact that we have saints in the church. It's not that we pray to them. They are there as a reminder of who they were and what they did and how we can be like them.

It doesn't bother me. The Roman Catholic faith—this is my faith and this is who I am. But that's who they are. The way I see it, the world is so diverse, it would be impossible to reach everyone with just one faith. I firmly believe that it's all the same faith—just manifested in different forms. And I believe that they all have the power to do some good in the long term. Unfortunately they get twisted around by fanatics.

I've Had Many Debates with Protestants

Carl, 18
Christian (Catholic)

I dated a Protestant girl once, and she took me to some sort of large retreat. There were a number of speakers, and they were holy rolling. People would come up on the altar and some guy would put his hands over people, and they would, like, collapse. At one point this guy with real big hands—he was always pointing and twirling his hands—he said, "I don't worship the saints. I'm not Catholic!" In the congregation, there was a definite approval of the statement.

Her father was a pastor. She told me on more than one occasion that her parents did not believe that Catholics were Christian. And I believe there was something about the pope being evil.

---

[17] Catholics have seven sacraments: baptism, reconciliation, the Eucharist or Holy Communion, confirmation, marriage, holy orders, and anointing of the sick. Most Protestants have two: baptism and communion.

I've definitely gotten, "Catholics will do anything for the pope." As soon as the pope says something, we prostrate ourselves and do it, without thinking.

I went to a public school. My friend was a nondenominational Protestant. We would have this continual banter. My position on the Protestant religion is that their theology is very loose and doesn't make a lot of sense to me. Protestants, to my knowledge, believe that you must accept Jesus as your savior before you die, otherwise you go to hell. And I would say, "What about stillborn babies? Or people who had never heard of Jesus Christ? Why are they condemned to hell?"

Catholics believe there is a period after you die when you have the opportunity to accept Jesus as your savior, and that takes care of things like the stillborn babies who never got baptized but died with original sin.

He would always come back with the point against Catholicism that we "worship graven images." We're not really praying to the saints. We're not worshipping the saints. We're not worshipping Mary. We're using them as some sort of conduit.

I've had many debates with Protestants, where there's always that snide remark about altar boys. There's all this sexual stuff coming to light and it unfortunately casts a pretty grim picture over all the priests. It seems that if you're not Catholic, it would be very easy to get the impression that that's what the bulk of Catholic priests are like.

I think that's very unfortunate and very untrue. I was an altar boy. I never had any awkward sexual experiences with my priests. The idea of priests being corrupt would never have entered my mind had it not been for the media. I definitely feel that it's blown out of proportion. I guess that's just the way that the media works. You never hear the heartwarming stories of a priest who helped a marriage stay together, or the story about a fundraiser that happened at a church, which are things that I experience all the time.

Intolerance includes a broad spectrum of acts including name-calling, harassment, and hate crimes. It's obvious that these types of acts are hurtful and often illegal.

Less obvious are acts that cause people to feel excluded or ignored.

They Would Just Assume Things

Abra, 20
Jewish (Reform)

My town is mostly white, upper middle class, and heavily Republican. In elementary school there were years when I was the only Jewish person in my class.

At school, people wouldn't be intolerant—they would just assume things. They wouldn't understand why I'd have to miss school for Jewish holidays. What would bother me is their not really caring enough to want to ask questions or to want to know. **Even though my school and my town made such a big deal out of promoting cultural diversity, a lot of times, socially, it was pretty popular to promote conformity.**

But I do feel like it's important to learn about somebody's culture first, so that they have a chance to explain how this is important in their life, before you just move past it and let it slip into the background.

The time when I became really involved in exploring my Jewish identity was in high school, when I joined the Reform youth movement. They had conferences every couple weeks, and we'd have workshops, sing, and have Shabbat celebrations.

I can clearly remember ninth grade, before I'd ever gone to NFTY. I went to see the movie *Titanic* on Christmas Eve with a Jewish friend of mine. I felt so alienated—to not be celebrating Christmas that night. I remember being in the movie theater and thinking, "This is so lonely. Why don't I just celebrate Christmas? Why do I have to be different?"

And then the next week, I went to my first conclave. I'd never been in a place where there were so many people with curly hair before. I was like, "These are my people, they understand me." And everything changed after that.

Throughout the country, the number of incidents involving harassment, discrimination, and violence against Muslims rose 15 percent from 2001 to 2002. In 2002, there were 602 of these incidents, according to the Council on American-Islamic Relations, an Islamic civil liberties group. After September 11 there was a large spike in the number of anti-Muslim, anti-Arab hate crimes nationwide.

Some prominent Christian leaders are partially to blame, says Mark Potok, of the Southern Poverty Law Center, an organization that monitors hate crime and promotes tolerance. For example, after September 11, evangelist Rev. Franklin Graham called Islam "a very evil and wicked religion." This type of rhetoric continues today, Potok says:

> *A lot of the big churches are driving anti-Muslim hatred. Some well-known preachers are standing at the pulpit and attacking Islam as a kind of satanic religion, a religion that promotes violence, a false religion, and so on. Those people are probably doing more harm than almost anyone.*

Hours after the September 11 terrorist attacks, an angry mob shouting anti-Arab and anti-Muslim insults gathered outside a mosque in the Chicago suburb of Bridgeview. The police had to be called in to protect the mosque and the Muslim religious school next door. I spoke with students at that school.

What Does It Have to Take for Me to Become an American?

Assia, 17; Hiba, 18; classmate who didn't want to be identified; Banan, 17

Assia: It was really bad after 9/11. I live a couple blocks down from the mosque. On September 11, we heard about the attacks on the radio on the way to school. We all went to classes, and about two hours later, students started getting dismissed. Parents were scared of repercussions to the school because everybody knows we're an Islamic school. Everybody left, and they closed down the school.

And at night, there were so many people gathered, and they were planning on coming into the neighborhood. They were driving down the street with American flags and saying, "Go back to where you came from!" and shouting out vulgarities and stuff, as if the American flag supports that. We had American flags hanging up at our homes, too.

I couldn't go to sleep. There was like beeping, shouting, and stuff. There was heightened security. The police had to stop anyone coming into the community unless you were a resident. There was a curfew.

I was like, "Why do people have to come straight to us? Look at this thing that just happened—why can't people just sit and reflect? Why do people have to take out their anger on us? Like we're not mourning September 11, too?"

Banan: There were people we know whose family members were in that building in New York—they were in the towers. And it's really, really frustrating when people just attack us and make us feel like, "You're not a part of us— you're not American."

I honestly had trouble trying to understand the hate crimes and attacks on Muslim-Americans. My parents were born in Jordan and Palestine, and I was born here. I have adopted many things from the American culture, including values of liberty, freedom, and advancement, as well as from my Middle-Eastern culture. Those values I cherish correspond to the values of my culture and more importantly my Islamic faith. Just because I am not white, or I dress differently, or hold a different faith than most Americans does not make me less American. When am I going to be looked at as an American?

Assia: Like really, what are we? You go back home, and they consider you an American, right? If we're not American—and we're not Palestinian, Jordanian, or Algerian—what are we?

Banan: Being born and raised in this country, we identify as being American. And when we are treated as outsiders or even terrorists, we fall into an identity crisis. I think what people have a hard time understanding is a person can be a Muslim and an American at the same time. I think most students felt aggravated and confused due to that.

Assia: At first you get mad. You're like, "Why are these people doing this?" And you understand that it's from ignorance, that people don't really know why they're doing it. They don't know who we are. If they really knew, I don't think that they'd be harassing us.

Hiba: I got a lot of stares because I wear the hijab outside of school at the mall, at grocery stores, whatever. All I could do is stare back and say, "What?" I was afraid that they were going to say something like, "Go back to your country," and I wouldn't know how to answer back.

Assia: After September 11 a lot of the Muslim women took off their scarves because they were so scared about being harassed. There were rumors of a Muslim woman in another state getting beaten because of her scarf. But I wasn't scared. I mean, this is who I am. I wear a scarf, accept me.

I guess I just want people to know that I'm just like you—you're just like me. I have morals. I have values. I cherish family. I think people like to think in their minds, you're different. You and me are not so different.

Banan: Every year, my family and I go to Jordan to visit our relatives. Sometimes my cousins and I have discussions about American foreign policy or cultural issues. I sense a difference in our way of thinking and outlook. When I come back to the U.S. I feel like people push me out, so I don't feel I belong here as much. We're kind of in the middle. **We don't fit under the category of first-generation immigrants nor under mainstream America. So we're just like a gap generation.**

It Was Just a Plane Full of Crazy People

Sarah, 21
Muslim

It really bothers me when I see things on television where they mention Islam in a negative manner, because Islam isn't negative. There are people who do things in the name of Islam that have nothing to do with Islam, and it's given off a negative image. I wish I could talk to every single person who thinks that Islam teaches war, fighting, and terrorism, but I can't.

The terrorist bombings of 9/11 were horrific. Everybody was in shock about that. But every time something like that happens it seems like Islam is brought in first. They say it was an Islamic fundamentalist who did this. It was just a plane full of crazy people—a plane full of people who were misinformed, misguided. I know they think they were right, and I know there are a lot of people who disagree with my views on that, but Islam does not teach violence. That's not to say you sit back and take anything. You're supposed to fight for your rights.

It's gotten better over the past three or four years. I think when President Clinton was in office, during Ramadan, they had an *iftar*, which is the breaking of the fast. They had that at the White House, and I was really impressed. When there were church bombings going on in the South four or five years ago, I remember hearing a speech where he said we have to protect "our churches, our temples, our mosques."

Things have changed. It's not such a Judeo-Christian country anymore. It really is a Judeo-Christian-Muslim country.

Racial Profiling Is Wrong

Arif, 19
Muslim

I don't go on airplanes often. But since September 11, when I did go on an airplane, I'm used to being taken aside, and they check my bags. That's not a problem. I understand that, given the situation at the time.

I work for a youth organization called Young Muslims. Essentially we focus on helping Muslim youth and teaching them the values of Islam. Last summer there was a group of seven of us from the Young Muslims group from Chicago. We were going to Mecca and Medina for 'umra. We had a stopover in Philadelphia, and we were going to New York. And then from New York, the next day, we were going on a flight to Saudi Arabia.

In Philadelphia we had to go on a different plane. We got on the airplane, and the pilot himself came back and took out five of us. He was like, "I don't feel comfortable with taking you on this airplane." And then they brought security, and we were taken off the airplane. And I said, "You missed two people."

The pilot was African-American. That's the sad thing about it—you would think that after what they've gone through, they would know that racial profiling is wrong.

It delayed the plane, and we had to get all our luggage from downstairs. They apologized and put us on a bus to go to the airport in New York. They didn't give us any reimbursement of our ticket or nothing. This is not how business works.

Bosnian Muslims say that they don't fit the stereotypical picture that most Americans have of a Muslim. First, they are not of Arab descent—only about 18 percent of the world's Muslims are Arabs.[18] Arabs are people who speak Arabic as their first language.

Nadia and Erina are good friends who met each other in their mosque's religious education program. Both of their families come from Bosnia and Herzegovina.

He Was Dissing My Religion

Nadia,* 12
Muslim
*not her real name

Some people—if you tell them that you're Muslim—they're like, "Yeah." And then they try to not talk to you anymore.

There was this girl in my class last year, and she was from Iraq. And she didn't feel like telling anybody because she felt that people weren't going to be her friends anymore. So she told me and she told this other girl, and the other girl told the whole school. And you could just see a difference in people. When they saw she was from Iraq, they kind of tried to stay away from her. Why do they do that? I mean, they're Christian—we don't stay away from them.

Sometimes I don't tell people I'm Muslim. But I should be able to tell people what I am.

---

[18] Islam follows Christianity as the religion with the most followers around the globe. Estimates of the number of Muslims worldwide range from 900 million to 1.3 billion, according to Adherents.com. Less than 20 percent of the world's Muslims are Arabs. Most Arab-Americans are Christians.

Erina,* 13
Muslim
*not her real name

In class we were learning about Islam. We went around the room and talked about our religion. If you wanted to say, you said. If you didn't, you said, "Pass." And I said my religion because I'm proud of it and there's nothing to be ashamed of. I pray and I learn suras,[19] and I do everything my mom tells me to because I want to respect my religion.

One day I brought in my scarf and I put it on, because I wanted to show them that there's different things people do in their religions. And everyone was like, "That's cool." They asked a lot of questions, they wanted to learn about it.

But like a week later, this one guy—for some reason he got mad at me, and he told me to "go back to Baghdad." That really made me mad. He was dissing my religion. I almost cried. Because, first of all, just because they're Muslim in Iraq doesn't mean I'm from there. And even if I was from there, so what?

I know that since the beginning of the war if you say that you're Muslim, and people over there in Iraq are Muslim, they'll think you're one of them. And they'll look at you in a whole different way.

I sat down and talked to him. **I said, "You know, I don't make fun of you. So don't make fun of me. And if I respect your religion, you should respect mine."** If you don't want to learn about it, then just don't say anything. It's better not to say anything than hurt somebody. And I told the teacher because that really made me mad. The teacher talked to him, and he got into trouble.

My best friend isn't the same religion as me; she's Polish [Christian]. And she respects me, I respect her. Right now, she's at school, too, learning about religion. She's learning about the same things as me, except she's Polish and I'm Bosnian.

Like when I was learning suras, she tested me on them so I could get better at it. If I said a word wrong, she would test me on it so I could get it. I love her for that.

---

[19]A sura is part (similar to a chapter) of the Qur'an.

In writing about people who have suffered acts of prejudice, I'm often inspired by their determination to fight back. You saw this in Erina. She confronted her tormentor and then reported him to the teacher. As you read more of these stories, you'll see other ways that people combat injustice.

People Were Putting the Religion on Trial

Kamran, 21
Muslim

In the wake of 9/11, my parents were really scared. My mom told me to shave my beard and not to talk about Islam in front of anybody. Many of my friends indicated that their families also reacted in the same way. There was this feeling of "Put aside your Islam, put aside your identity for a while, so that you don't receive any of this violent backlash." The backlash was occurring, but it wasn't as dramatic and widespread as many were making it out to be. As time went on, people stopped being so paranoid.

As an American and as a Muslim, I was terribly shocked by what had happened. What was even more disheartening was the fact that it was being linked to people who supposedly had the same faith as I do. It was scary to see that someone who believes in some of the same things I do could twist and pervert it to fit their own political, quasi-religious agendas and pull off something like that. At the religious school I went to, I was never taught a political ideology or to have hatred for anyone else.

On the other hand, I also felt more sympathetic to situations going on across the world, because as an American, I've always felt sheltered. We have this aura that nothing can happen to us. It really opened up my eyes and my heart to the plight of people in other nations and what they must go through every day. I felt the need for Americans at large to be aware about what's going on around the world. We can't continue to live the sheltered lives we've lived.

On a third level, I was feeling some resentment and a little bit of confusion as to why people began to associate this with mainstream Islam. In other situations—like with Timothy McVeigh—nobody mentioned his religion or his race.[20] You'd think that people would judge you for what you are and not for what other people have done. And I found it really antithetical to the American way, which is to have equality and fair treatment of everyone.

"We'll Be Your Shield"

It seemed to me that people were putting the religion on trial. It seemed to me that people were being unfair toward Islam, especially the mainstream media. You had all sorts of people—like these political writers, Steve Emerson, Ann Coulter, and David Horowitz—speaking a bunch of nonsense. I felt that people were letting their biases dictate how they wanted to view this religion and a people.

As far as the reaction at University of Illinois at Chicago, it was very positive. There were one or two isolated events of people being harassed. But that was actually off campus by the local people, people who live in the projects over here. As far as positive feedback, the chancellor of the university herself extended her support to us. We had a lot of students come up to us and say, "We support you during these tough times," "We understand that this is not representative of your religion," "We apologize in advance for anything people might say." It was a refreshing surprise.

With the younger generation, people aren't necessarily buying into what's put out on mainstream media. People are willing to be open and look at issues critically. I knew that there were people who wouldn't necessarily buy into the messages being sent out after 9/11 about "Islam is the enemy."

Overall, I think the reaction of the American community was more positive than negative toward the Muslim community. I heard that Americans were forming circles around local mosques, saying, "We'll be your shield," when there was vandalism in the wake of 9/11. But there's still a lot more work to be done, especially from our government and our leaders.

I think that many non-Muslim-Americans have the idea that one has to be Muslim or American—you can't be both. The basic principles that Muslims believe in are the same principles that this country was founded on—justice, family values, caring for your neighbor, things like that. To be a good Muslim, we're told that you have to respect the laws of your country, and be model

---

[20] McVeigh, a European-American, set off the explosives that destroyed an Oklahoma City federal office building and killed 168 men, women, and children. He was executed in June 2001.

citizens, and that you must give more than you receive. I don't think it's incompatible to be Muslim and American.

I think it's just a lack of proper information given to people about what Islam is all about. For too long, there have been these proverbial veils over Islam. Hopefully, in the near future, these veils can be gradually lifted and people can be given true information about what the religion is all about, what Muslims are all about, what they believe in—and to understand that we don't have this world-domination agenda like some evangelicals are saying. We're just human beings like everybody else.

Secular Islam

Oz, 20
Muslim

I was born to Muslim parents in Ankara. The approach to Islam is very different in urban Turkey. People approach religion as something that is just faith; practice is no longer that important.

There is a social role that it plays. When I was growing up, I didn't go to a mosque on a regular basis. But three or four times in my life, on a religious holiday, my dad would take me to the mosque. We'd go there to meet other people and celebrate. Even when it comes to fasting, which is part of Ramadan—that was never an issue in my household. We did it for health reasons mostly. There was no pressure. This is typical in urban Turkey.

You can find a lot of really different sects and practices of Islam in Turkey. Some people pray through singing or playing instruments. There are the whirling dervishes. I'm sure it's hard to see that kind of innovative approach to the religion as you get closer to the original source of it.

Not many people know the difference between the Turkish tradition of Islam and the more unsecular ways. They just assume that you're a part of this one big group. When you say you're a Muslim, they don't want to inquire, they don't want to get into the details, they don't want to know how much of a Muslim you are. They don't even have an idea about the degrees or differences or variances in

Islam. What they see is a bunch of guys burning the American flag. And the image is not appealing to them, so they just cast you off when you say you're a Muslim.

Gallup polls show that anti-Semitism has dropped markedly in the United States during the past sixty-five years. In 1937, only 46 percent of Americans polled by Gallup said they would vote for a qualified presidential candidate who is Jewish. In 1999, 92 percent of those polled responded that way. In 2004, Joe Lieberman, a Jewish-American and U.S. Senator from Connecticut, sought the Democratic nomination for president.

However, in 2002, there were 1,559 incidents—threats, assaults, vandalism—that targeted Jews and Jewish institutions in the U.S., according to the Anti-Defamation League, an organization that tracks anti-Semitic incidents worldwide. Since 2000 and the beginning of the current Palestinian uprising against Israel, some Jews noticed increased hostility against Jews on college campuses.

Most of the Jews I spoke with had never had an anti-Semitic encounter. Growing up in West Rogers Park, home to the largest concentration of Chicago's Orthodox Jews, Ephraim says he was vaguely aware that anti-Semitism existed "over there."

On Friday, July 2, 1999, he was one of nine people, including six Jews, who were shot and wounded in drive-by shootings in Chicago and nearby areas. Two people were killed. Minorities were targeted—Jews, blacks, and Asian Americans. The twenty-one-year-old who committed the shootings and then killed himself was a member of a white supremacist anti-Semitic group based in southern Illinois.

Although incidents like this are extremely rare, Ephraim says it opened his eyes. Here's his story.

You Always Know That There Are People Out There That Hate You

Ephraim, 19
Jewish (Orthodox)

Me and my friend were walking to evening prayers. A light blue Ford Taurus pulled up to the side of us and stopped. We're like, he's looking for a parking spot, or he might have dropped something and stopped to pick it up. So we didn't pay attention to him.

The next thing I knew, I saw two flashes in the corner of my eye. I heard two gunshots. The second shot hit me in the leg, two inches below the knee. Once he hit me, he burned rubber and drove off. Me and my friend looked at each other and we were like, "What the heck was that?" So I kept on walking. My leg felt weird. I lifted up my pants, and I saw a hole the size of a dime and blood was gushing out.

I turned to my friend. I was like, "I'm shot! I'm shot!" He just looked at me like, whoa! He goes to a house and tells the person I was shot. They called the police. I was in shock. My leg was just basically dead. It didn't start hurting until three or four hours later.

At the hospital, they bandaged up my leg. I had a hairline fracture. I couldn't walk on it for three months. They didn't take the bullet out. Since it's inside my leg, the bone will heal over it. For the first two years, I felt it in there. Whenever I exercised really hard, I would really feel it.

Six people were shot—three people were shot on my block. Almost twenty people were shot at.

I Never, Never Thought It Could Happen to Me

I always heard about these things, but never, never thought that it could happen to me. It hadn't crossed my mind that there are people out there who don't even know me, who want me dead. In the Jewish community, you always know that there are people out there that hate you. You're taught this. You're taught about the Holocaust, about Nazis killing Jews like they are nothing. You always hear about the Ku Klux Klan, neo-Nazis, all those kinds of people. You hear about it, but you don't take it to heart. You always think it's over there—it's not over here.

My freshman year of high school, one time we were talking about anti-Semitism in America. I remember the teacher said, "If you people think that there's no anti-Semitism in America, you have another think coming." But I didn't take it to heart.

And when that happened to me, it hit me like a brick wall, like a smack in the face. It's like this whole big world became so small, like you could fit it in your hands. Like everything seemed close, and I wasn't sheltered anymore. When it does happen to you, you take on a new way of looking at things.

It's not every day that some guy comes into your neighborhood and starts shooting people. West Rogers Park is a mainly Jewish area, but there are a lot of different races, a lot of different cultures. It's a nice neighborhood. The past four years, we had a couple incidents. Two Palestinian teenagers asked a rabbi if he was a rabbi. He said, "Yeah." And they pulled out a gun and unloaded a clip. Thank God, none of the bullets hit him, but his car was riddled with bullet holes.

When I was in an elementary day school, one time there were swastikas spray-painted on the walls. When you're walking down the street, someone would stop a car and yell something and drive away. One time when I was ten, someone threw a rock at my head—they missed me. There was a time when my brother came home and his pants were all dirty. I said, "What happened?" He said some guy said, "You f-ing—" and not a nice word for a Jew, and threw yogurt at him.

These things are not unheard of—but not common. Like once a year, something like that might happen. There's different ways it affects people. Some people get real down and depressed. They feel like they can't go out. And it takes a little while for them to get over it. Some people get extremely angry. They are outraged and want to find some of these people and beat them up. Other people just deal with it and go on.

The way I was brought up is, if you see something like that happen, you try to stop it, whatever it costs. But you cannot let it get to you. I remember telling my father when I was in the hospital, "I think I should be afraid, but I'm not. I'm not going to let this stop me." I could look at this and say, "I'm shot,

I can't go outside, I have to wear a bulletproof vest and a body of armor to go outside." Or you could be like, "You know what? They shot me. I'm not dead. I'm just going to walk in the street to show you that you have to do more than that to take me down."

Some of my friends, once they saw I was OK, they started spewing jokes—left and right, crack after crack after crack. You can either mope about it or laugh about it. Which would you rather do? I think laughing about it was better for me.

I'm Always Going to Be Jewish

After this happened, I did a lot of interviews. Someone asked me if my faith was shaken by this. And I said, "Not at all. Not only has it not shaken my faith, it made my faith stronger." I wanted everybody to know that I'm still Jewish. I'm always going to be Jewish, and that this wasn't going to make me think about changing that.

You can look at it as: how can God let such a horrible thing happen? Or you can look at it as: God saved me. If it was two inches higher, my kneecap would have been blown off. If I was two seconds later, I might never have seen it. I believe every little thing that happens, happens for a reason, and I'm a very, very big believer in God.

So whenever something bad happens in the world and people say, "How could God let that happen?" I say, "I don't know, but I think God knows a little bit more than you do. And I think that he knows what's better for us. It might look horrible, but you don't see the big picture. We can't see the big picture, so we just gotta believe that God is good and he knows what he's doing."

We Don't Control America

Darcy, 23
Jewish (Modern Orthodox)

When I was eight, I was playing violin, and I went to a young musicians' summer camp with my parents. I wasn't going to services on Sunday, and this twelve-year-old boy asked me why, and I said, "I'm Jewish." And he just went off for about half an hour about how damned my soul was since Jesus didn't die for my sins. He said unless I converted, my whole family would burn in the fires of hell for eternity. It was not a pleasant thing to be told when you were eight, but it didn't really bother me. My reaction was to lecture him on the erroneousness of that idea.

I get strange things all the time. People are like, "Oh, you're Jewish. Is it true that Jews only have sex through a small hole in a sheet?" No, that's actually against Jewish law. I had someone come up to me and say, "So you're Jewish, right? I heard that Jews are supposed to have sex before they get married and they're really into orgies?" No.

It's really bizarre. Sometimes it's just innocent questions; people don't know better. A Jewish girlfriend of mine was asked if it's true that Jews freeze the placentas of their babies and then eat them. No. But there are definitely versions of the blood libel still around—the Christian blood libels that Jews use the blood of Christian children to make their matzo for Passover. There are similar stories still around that disturb people and get them very angry with Jews.

I've met a lot of anti-Semites who are very enthusiastic about just how evil Jews are. If you're Orthodox Jewish, it's impossible to not know about this. Some days there will be graffiti sprayed on your synagogue, and then the police will hang around for the rest of the day to make sure there are no problems. There will be regular warnings like, "The police received a threat against a synagogue, be careful, consider staying home if you don't have to go somewhere," et cetera.

In America, they complain that we control all the money of the world— just ridiculous stuff. People are convinced that I can do whatever I want because I have unlimited resources. I'm Jewish, so I must be incredibly wealthy. No, actually I'm not. I'm at school on a scholarship.

I have a classmate who is Egyptian. She came with me to synagogue once and was looking through the prayer book, which is in Hebrew and English. She was looking for the part where it says we should kill all the Arabs, because that's what she was always taught.

But there isn't anything in the prayer book or anything else about that because Jews don't believe that. We don't teach our children to hate Arabs or that they, or any other non-Jews, must die.

She also thinks that Jews rule the U.S., which a lot of people think. We don't control America. In fact, until very recently, in many ways we were very similar to blacks. It was fashionable to dislike Jews. We got blackballed from country clubs. If you look at charters for covenant-controlled communities, the old charters will actually list in their rules: "No blacks, no Jews. Mow your lawn once a week." They just put it in like it was a very normal thing.

"There's Something about the Jews"

Miriam, 22
Jewish (Orthodox)

Last year I tutored at this nursing school. This woman was from Guatemala. I'm sure she's educated, but she didn't speak English. My job was to teach her enough English so she could pass the test to get in. One day she said, "Miriam, are you Jewish?" I said, "Yeah." She said, "You know how I knew? Because you're very smart and you dress modestly." Then she said, "The Jews are the people of God—it says so in my Bible. That's why they're very smart and wealthy."

All Jews Are . . .

I didn't know what to say. If you're Jewish, there is definitely an emphasis on being smart and succeeding in school. If people think that, then OK. But it's a problem to think that all Jews are wealthy when they're not. I was in Argentina last quarter. They have this huge economic crisis and a lot of extreme poverty. Synagogues are feeding lots and lots of hungry people who are Jews. No one can pay tuition anymore at the Jewish schools. Anti-Semitism is more of an issue there. A woman from Uruguay told a friend of mine that the Jews run everything in Argentina.

People's willingness to believe things like that is weird. That's where I think stereotypes become a problem. It's not OK to say, "All Jews are wealthier," or "The Jews run things," or "There's something about the Jews."

Once someone was saying that the Jewish community has a bigger voice in America than the Muslim community. And I said that Muslims just haven't been here for so long, and that in fifty years, we'll see if it will still be true. I think the Muslim community in America is starting out in a very similar way that the Jewish community started out. Of course, these are generalizations, but they're immigrants, they work very hard, they're really into education, and they make sure to send their kids to college. But there are some people who can't stomach that kind of answer, and they say, "No, there's something about the Jews—they act so organized, and they're so . . . " whatever.

There is a willingness to explain away anti-Jewish remarks that I find really troubling, particularly in academia, particularly in leftist circles. There is a tendency to try to apologize for really violent things said about Jews in a lot of Arab countries, such as, "Oh, they just don't know," or "It's because of what happened in Palestine."

It *is* because of what's happening in Palestine and Israel to a certain extent, but that's not enough of a reason to say that Jews use Muslim blood in their whatever. There was one case on an American university campus where a political student group put up posters that showed cans labeled "Palestinian baby meat, slaughtered according to Jewish rites," or something like that.

Evangelism

And then you have the Christian right. I grew up in Boston and now live here, so they're just not real for me. But they're real in the rest of the country, and that's sort of scary—their willingness to evangelize, to believe that they are so right that they can tell other people what to believe.

There are people on this campus who think it's their duty to evangelize Jews, which I find personally offensive. I find it very disrespectful. There are these organizations that are set up to convert Jews, like Jews for Jesus. They come here and ask people who are obviously Jewish, "Are you satisfied with your religion?" or "How does it feel to be in a religion without salvation?"

In general, I find evangelism a little bit offensive. But when it's targeted at someone, as if to say that you, specifically, are worse than anybody else—that's really disrespectful.

MY FAITH JOURNEY

I Think I Was Always Muslim

A former Christian describes events that led him to convert to Islam, although he was forced to practice his new faith in secret. Gerald is one of many African-Americans who call themselves Muslims. An estimated one-third of all Muslims in the U.S. are of African-American descent.

Gerald (Jihad), 21
Muslim

I grew up in probably one of the worst neighborhoods in Chicago. This area has been marked with a long history of violence, particularly with the drug surge that happened in the '80s. That's when the neighborhood really started down.

My entire family is Christian. The family never went to church on a regular basis. There was always the concept that church and God can be everywhere, not just within a built sanctuary. My mom had a lot of gospel music she played in the house, particularly on Sundays when she would clean up or cook.

I was more interested than anyone else, so I'd go to church. I knew I was Christian. I knew that I believed in God. I knew that God is everywhere. I sensed that God had done some wondrous things for me. Even though I grew up in this area, I wasn't caught into gang violence or drug selling. I did very well in school.

About the time I got to middle school, I had a heightened sense of spirituality and I wanted to know who God is and who all the people who are distinguished in the Bible were. I read this version of the Bible called the Living Bible. A family friend gave it to me. The English was not technical but straightforward. It had pictures. It was really cool. So I would read the Bible every day. . . .

There's a concept in Islam that everyone is born Muslim—not necessarily meaning that they acknowledge Islam, but they acknowledge that there's one God. In fact, Abraham is considered the first Muslim. He was the one who submitted to the first true God. I think I was always Muslim even when I was

Christian—there were little small things. Like I never cared for pork, I've always been a veggie-grain person. I was always a person of nature.

Questioning Christianity

I questioned Christianity quite early. I think the first major thing was how Jesus was regarded as being the Father, the Son, and the Holy Spirit—the whole trinity concept. Above all, the trinity was the one thing that really perplexed me. The famous quote where Jesus is on the cross and he says, "Oh my God, why has thou forsaken me?" That struck me because I couldn't see Jesus crying out like that in such agony, especially if he is supposed to be on par with God himself.

As I started to learn about other denominations of Christianity, I learned that all the Bibles are not the same. The Catholic Bible has extra books. And the *Book of Mormon*—they're supposed to be Christians, but their Bible is totally different. I remember visiting Rockome Gardens, an Amish community in Illinois, and they have a totally different book. Also, I learned that there are still books being discovered—there's the Gospel of Barnabas. And words that once appeared in earlier King James versions do not appear today; words have been deleted and changed within the Bible. I researched this by comparing the Bible I owned to a 1920 copy found at the Harold Washington Library. I concluded that the Bible was not authentic and to be wary of it.

Then another aspect of Christianity that really perplexed me was "catching the Holy Ghost." Supposedly, when you get riled up with God and his words—it's usually through song or just preaching—you catch the Holy Ghost.[21] And you become so energetic that you dance and shout and jump.

I decided on my sixteenth birthday to get baptized. When I got baptized, me and all the other people who got baptized were supposed to try to speak in tongues—that's part of catching the Holy Spirit. One of the sisters instructed us about how to do it. She said, "Don't force it. Just try to feel it. Continuously say 'Jesus.' And if you start stuttering, or it becomes very inaudible, do not alter your voice. Just keep along with it."

---

[21] Some Christians, especially Pentecostals, believe that evidence that the Holy Spirit (God) has been received is "speaking in tongues," or speaking in a language unknown to the speaker.

And I tried to do it. I said I would not get up until I felt it. I just kept saying, "Jesus, Jesus, Jesus." But I wasn't feeling it at all. I wondered, "What's the purpose of it?" It was quite weird.

Nation of Islam

One day my best friend, Tyrone, gave me a call and said, "Guess what, man? I joined the Nation of Islam." [22] Me and Tyrone lived close by, so we'd take the bus home. We used to get into these discussions about Christianity and Islam. And he would feed me his Nation of Islam brand of Islam.

The Nation of Islam is totally different from orthodox Islam. I remember one story that showed me that the Nation was not legit. One part of the story is about some mad scientist named Yaqub who believes that all people at the beginning of time were black. The whites were banished to go to the north, what is now Europe, and the Chinese and all Asians to Asia. He said something to the effect that, "This is how white people became white, how Chinese people became yellow." And there's something about a spaceship. It was really crazy and didn't make sense.

One day Tyrone did not speak to me at all, totally ignored me. I said, "Are you OK? What's the matter?" He finally explains to me, "Hey, I can't be friends with you no more." He points out this verse in the Qur'an. The verse pretty much said that the Christians and Jews war against you and thus you don't befriend them. It's a controversial verse now.

I was like, "This is something that happened thousands of years ago. I've done nothing to you." He continued to be my friend. **This is one of those things that a lot of people do, both Muslims and non-Muslims. If they read a verse from the Qur'an, they take it verbatim. It can be good, but it's also dangerous because there's a reason that the verse reads as it does, why it was revealed.**

Finding Islam in My Own Way

There are experiences that I reflect upon as eventual steps toward finding Islam in my own way. In third grade I decided to write a paper on Malcolm X and I got an A-plus on it. He was the first person I considered my role model. In the sixth grade, my mom took me and my sister to see the movie *Malcolm X*.

---

[22] A minority of African-American Muslims belong to the Nation of Islam, currently led by Minister Louis Farrakhan.

The opening scene is where Malcolm was on his hajj, and he's in the mosque in Saudi Arabia, and he recites the first sura of the Qur'an. They had an English translation across the screen, and the words were so beautiful, it made me cry. That just stuck with me.

I went to Lindblom Technical, a perennial academic powerhouse in Chicago. I had to do a research paper in my AP English class. I went to my neighborhood library. As soon as I walked in I saw four copies of the *Autobiography of Malcolm X*. The book is about Malcolm's life. But he points out a lot of things that are not only wrong with the black community, but also with Christianity and life in American society. And he points out how Islam addresses those problems.

It was influential. A lot of things that went on in Malcolm's life were almost equivalent to mine, so I related to him on so many levels. He talked about how he joined NOI—Nation of Islam—how he got it moving, how conflicts started happening, how he went to the Middle East and on his hajj, and then how he went from the Nation into orthodox or universal Islam. That book is what really got me going, "Wow, Islam is really something!"

Tyrone was fortunate enough to have money to go on a trip to North Africa with his family in '97. He comes back from North Africa and goes to one of his NOI sessions. He calls me and he says, "Man, I've been kicked out the Nation." He tells me it was like a Q-and-A session, and he stood up and asked, "If we're truly Muslims, then why are we not practicing the real Islam?"

I guess he went through the same experiences Malcolm went through when he went to North Africa and saw that Islam is not just for blacks—it's for all humanity. And some of the nicest people you can ever meet are people of white skin, blond hair, blue eyes, and all that. Because of the question Tyrone asked, they saw it as insubordination. For that, he was kicked out of the Nation. I was infuriated.

Tyrone befriended this Palestinian storeowner. This guy started to give me literature about Islam. I took it and read it. It led me to continue researching and finding out what Islam is. Then Tyrone and me would go to the library and try to find books on Islam. Tyrone became a Muslim.

MY FAITH JOURNEY

Secret Faith

On Wednesday, April 22, 1998, I became a Muslim. I grabbed Tyrone and said, "I think I'm ready to become Muslim." He teaches me the shahadah, which is the declaration of faith, considered the first pillar of Islam. The shahadah is said in Arabic. The English translation is "There is no god but God, and Muhammad is his prophet and messenger." After I say this, Tyrone says, "You're now Muslim."

I was living Islam in secret. I was praying in secret. I already knew how my family was with me just *being Gerald*. The friction was already in the household. I assumed that they wouldn't accept me being a Muslim.

One day I'm in my room, I'm praying. I heard my mom calling me. In Islam you do not break your prayer for anyone—no one comes before God. Then my father calls me. He kept calling me. He pounds on the door. I was still praying. He comes in and sees me praying. I stop and look up, and he has this look on his face. He is so-o-o upset. He's like, "You practicing that stuff, aren't you?" We get into this argument, because I didn't ask him if I could become Muslim. Finally, he said, "You can believe, but you can't practice in here. Anything that represents Islam can't come into the house." To just have some peace, I said, "OK, fine." I knew that wasn't going to happen.

One day I got home and my father's like, "Where have you been? Who did you go with?" My father said, "Bring your stuff down, all your salaam stuff. I'm going to throw it away."

He had my Qur'an. He had my books. He had my literature, my prayer rug. I was very hurt by it. I didn't do anything wrong, and here I am being punished.

A concept shared in both Christianity and Islam is that the best people are always the ones who go through hardship and tests. That's what got me through a lot of hard times.

Monday after graduation, I left for an internship in Colorado. My father told me to pack everything. Before I left I said, "Can I have my Muslim things?" He's like, "You won't be able to come back in this house if you bring that back with you." I was like "fine" and left.

I graduated with a 4.5 GPA on a 4-point scale. But the schools I applied to didn't offer me any money at all despite my grades and extracurricular activities. I almost cried knowing I was going to UIC. I just wanted to get away—get out of the state, the region.

The second or third week of school, all the student organizations set up booths for students to sign up. I came across the Muslim Student Association table. I signed up. There's a lot of Muslims on campus. But I felt so disconnected from them; I didn't feel them reach out to me. If I knew someone was Muslim, I'd say, "Assalaamu ala ikum."[23] It's mandatory for all Muslims. Unfortunately, no one ever returned salaam to me. And it made me feel even more alone.

One day, it was still warm and I was wearing shorts and a T-shirt. I saw a sign that said "jumma" [Friday prayer service]. I ran upstairs. I was so happy. Everybody just looked. I was the only black guy. I totally stood out. I sat down and prayed. I got up and put on my shoes, and this brother came out. He's like, "You're not supposed to wear that to jumma." I was like, "I didn't know jumma was held here. If I did, I would have dressed more conservatively." And my feelings were hurt—like I can't do anything right.

Unfortunately, a lot of new Muslims come and then leave. It's because people who are already Muslim are so hard on them. These people assert the fact that they were born Muslim and that they know better than you.

So these two brothers, a Pakistani and a Somali, they came and introduced themselves to me and said, "The eighth floor is the hangout spot for the MSA, for the brothers. We study there, we eat there, we chill there, play games there. Why don't you come up?" I went up with those two and I was hooked.

Since then, I've learned a lot about Islam. I was immersed. I had all the lectures, discussions, conversations. And these people really embraced me. There was this other guy, Carlos, he's Mexican and Italian. He became Muslim a year or two before I did. At the time, I was struggling with money. He asked me if I was hungry. He asked me if I had any money. I was like, "No, I'm fine, I'll be cool." Carlos just went in his pocket and gave me $10. He folded it in my hand. And that's how those brothers were. There's so much love I got from them.

I feel that God has saved me from a lot of trying times and he was quite evident in my life. I was given people who truly love me, people who respect me and want to see me succeed.

---

[23] Peace be with you.

Where Is God?

Does God exist? If so, why is there so much suffering and injustice in the world? Does science and technology trump religion? Why do I believe what I believe?

Most of the people I interviewed said they've questioned their beliefs and their faith. For some of them, this period of doubt lasted several months. For others, it lasted much longer.

James Fowler, author of the groundbreaking book Stages of Faith: The Psychology of Human Development *(San Francisco: Harper, 1995), has studied faith development in the lives of hundreds of people of all ages. He theorizes that people can pass through up to six stages of faith as they grow from child to adult. Many only make it through three or four.*

The transition times, or the time people take to move from one stage to another, "are as important as the more stable times" and can last anywhere from two-and-a-half to five years in young people, he says.

"Doubt and struggle aren't necessarily rejecting one's faith, but perhaps longing for a more intimate relationship with the Holy," says Fowler.

"It takes courage to acknowledge doubt and to wrestle with your beliefs," says Sharon Daloz Parks, author of Big Questions, Worthy Dreams: Mentoring Young Adults in Their Search for Meaning, Purpose, and Faith *(San Francisco: Jossey-Bass, 2000). "It's much easier to settle for a fierce unquestioned belief."*

Doubt presents opportunity to grow in your faith, she adds, "to step into a larger faith, a more adequate faith, and a more spacious and profound way of seeing."

In this chapter you'll read about young people who grappled with big questions about their faith.

Shaky Waters

Hesed, 14
Christian (United Methodist)

I'm walking this line between faith and reason,
Afraid to cross,
Afraid to jump,
Staying in the security of no man's land.
I walk this line, all the time wondering why I'm still following,
Step by step, one foot following the other,
When reason has been whispering in my ear, proclaiming what it has to offer,
All the things I desire—
REALITY, CERTAINTY, STABILITY,
All that I have always clung to,
And yet, I'm still here, stuck in NEUTRAL.

Faith beckons to me, pulling at my head to turn and cast my sight
On the river of uncertainty,
Rocks and rapids, sharp twists and turns,
And my eyes close in fear, and I quickly turn away.

My eyes open, and they follow the path that this line makes
Until it loudly disappears into the horizon.
It echoes off my surroundings, straight to my heart.
Suddenly,
I want to drive out of this cage of security, to toss instinct and logic to the wind.
I close my eyes and cast away sight.
I take the deepest breath I have ever taken
As I let go of firm ground,
And dive into shaky waters.

How Do I Know This Is the Real Truth?

The poem is about confusion about religion. I was vague about a lot of things at the time when I wrote it. I knew I was Christian, and I knew I believed it. But I was like, "How do I know for sure? How do I know this is the real truth?" We claim Jesus died to save the world. Buddhism has Buddha, and Islam has Muhammad. But they have basic similarities, and if they're all similar, which one do I choose?

Ever since I was born I've had a religion, but I haven't really had a faith until confirmation. Your parents baptized you when you were little. You're confirming the promise that they made at your baptism when they spoke for you. You're affirming that you believe what they did for you then. Basically that's what confirmation is. You go in front of the congregation and you say a statement of faith. And the pastor might ask you to read the Beatitudes, or some text.

I didn't have any requirements. We had classes once a week for a couple months. A lot of the assignments were like reading the Bible and meditating on it and trying to figure it out. And that opened up a lot of doors on what I believed in and why.

What About Other Religions?

After confirmation I was getting stronger in the faith, but I still thought about it and said, "Well, what about other religions? Are they fake? And if they are, why are there millions of Muslims around the world who pray to Allah five times a day? And why are there Buddhists who make Buddhism their faith? Why do I think this one faith is real?"

And basically, to me, I just get a feeling. It's really hard to explain. **Christianity just feels right to me.** I go to church, and I see the cross, and we're at prayer—it feels right. And I can honestly say that I feel the presence of God in that place. And for me, Christianity is the religion where I feel that. To me that's basically what faith is—to just believe in what you think is right. And this is right for me.

Now I'm really secure in what I believe. And I don't know if it's wrong to say it—since I'm a Christian and we're supposed to go out and save the world and convert people to Christianity—but I truly do believe that there are a lot of people who feel that their religion, whether it be Islam, or Buddhism, or Hinduism, is right for them. And I don't see anything wrong with that. I'm not saying those are the right faiths, but you just get a feeling when something is right for you.

Carl, a Catholic, says he grew up in his church. He writes how habit and upbringing—rather than a deeply felt spiritual connection—are at the core of his religious identity.

Untouched

Carl, 18
Christian (Catholic)

The woman's daughter wasn't developing in the womb, and through a combination of science and prayer the baby overcame heart and lung complications. Not an eloquent speaker, but standing before the podium in my church, on the granite altar before countless parish families, she cried—and so did we.

So naturally I reflect: Prayer helped her through the crisis, but more in the "mind-over-matter" sense. It improved her mood and her expectations, which therefore altered the outcome of her crisis—

The story was still very touching.

I believe in my religion, my God, and my Church, but I cannot classify myself as a "believer." My mother would simply say I have not yet been "touched." In my eyes, I'm simply practical: Jesus lived; we have the artifacts to prove it. Had Jesus been a poet, he would have rivaled the greats. He could manipulate words to corner malicious pharisees at a level that was, for all intents and purposes, Divine. So naturally, I respect him.

From fourth grade, I was an altar boy. Then I was the layperson chosen to proclaim scripture passages at mass, and I read the petitions and welcomed the congregation, as well as any newcomers or visitors, to our parish. I have held high marks with my church since I was quite young. I maintain the Church holds great power and is generally a positive formative force for the community, but I don't pray outside of mass, and I never rely on divine intervention.

With my adoration for the Man of Nazareth, for the community of the Church, and for the strength of religion all included, I accept Jesus as my savior. My love of his words does not, however, explain my worship. I prostrate myself before statues of the Christ man only because I have held high marks for so long. I worship for the same reason so many practical, thinking, un-"touched," holding-high-mark Catholics do: because we were raised to do so.

Many of the people I interviewed had explored or studied faiths other than the one in which they were raised. But few approached this task with the curiosity and intensity of Qasim. His inquiry into other beliefs and other ways of worship did not diminish his Islamic faith. It strengthened it.

You Shouldn't Be Muslim Just Because You Were Born into It

Qasim, 20
Muslim (Ahmadi)

I was a cocky little kid. I used to think that Islam was the right way and everyone else was wrong. That's when my dad encouraged me to study different religions. He saw I was getting really arrogant. He said, "You shouldn't be Muslim just because you were born into it. You should know why you believe in your religion."

So during the past three or four years, I've been studying every religion under the sun—Judaism, Christianity, Islam, Hinduism, Buddhism, Jainism, Taoism, Zoroastrianism. I even studied the Australian aborigines for a while. You'd be fascinated by how similar Native American religions are to Christianity, Islam, and Judaism.

I read the Qur'an. I read the Bible—the Old Testament, the New Testament. I read the gospels of Thomas and Barnabas [24]—and saw what they had to say. I studied books written by Muslim scholars, Christian scholars, one by a Jewish scholar—my comparative religions teacher is actually a rabbi. I studied books written by atheists. If they think God doesn't exist, I wanted to see what they had to say.

When you go to study a new religion, you go there with the intention of finding the ultimate truth. To do that you've got to do two things: First, you have to pray, because God could come out himself and say, "Here I am," but if your heart isn't open to it, then you're not going to accept it. Second of all, you need to let go of all the biases you had before.

When I studied Christianity, I had a bias that there's no way that Jesus could be the literal Son of God. But I threw that out. I thought, "OK, let's assume that he is the literal Son of God. How do I feel about this? Does it agree

---

[24] The gospels of Thomas and Barnabas are the two gospels that aren't included in the Bible.

with science? Does it make logical sense for God to have a literal, physical son?" And for me the answer was no.

I did let go of all biases when I studied Judaism. I thought, "Look they're still waiting for the Messiah. How does Judaism support the idea that a messiah hasn't come yet?" I read their argument; I saw what they had to say.

When I studied Hinduism, they talked about Krishna as God, Krishna being the manifestation of several different gods, and the idea of reincarnation. I thought, "Does that make sense to me? Does it make sense in my heart? Does it make sense in my mind?"

If you look at Islam, Christianity, and Judaism—they all teach the same basics. It's just when you get to the higher-up level that the dogma is so completely different. It makes you wonder how this happened. But throughout time there have been additions and subtractions here and there, and before you know it, they're completely different religions. Now I understand where some other religions strayed from the paths of their true teachings.

For example, we believe that the message that Christ brought was the truth and what you hear today includes changes, additions, and subtractions. We're not talking paragraphs taken out—but entire books put in or chopped out. That's one of the things that bother me about the Bible.

When you study religion, subject it to two different criteria. One, does it satisfy your heart? Does it morally make sense to you? For example, Christianity just didn't make moral sense to me—that God would banish his children to hell forever.[25] How could a loving God throw them in hell forever for the mistakes of a short forty, fifty, sixty, seventy years? Eternity is a long time compared with that. What if I died right now? I know I've done wrong.

In Islam, hell is not eternity, it's temporary. Hell is a place of purification. If your soul has a cancer in it, then hell is basically a hospital to get that cancer out until you're ready to accept God. The Qur'an says that to get into heaven, you have to believe in God, believe in the Day of Judgment, and you've got to help mankind or do good deeds. You're not just going to be judged on what religion you are. It boils down to what kind of person you are in this life. If you're a good person, you're going to go to heaven.

---

[25] The belief that God banishes sinners to hell for eternity is not taught or accepted by all Christians. For example, many Roman Catholics believe in a state called purgatory, where people who commit lesser sins are purified before going to heaven.

Truth

I believe in a day of judgment. I believe in a day when I will stand before God and I'm going to be held accountable for the good deeds that I did and the sins that I committed in this life. It's not going to be my dad standing there answering for me. So whatever religion I am, I want to be able to answer.

Let's say Islam is not the ultimate truth. Then when I stand before God, I will tell him, "You gave me an intellect, a great intellect. Thank you. I used it to the best of my ability. And if I didn't arrive at the conclusion that is the ultimate truth, basically I did my best." That's all God asks of us is to do our best. In the search for eternal truth—whatever you feel that may be—whether you arrive at Christianity, Islam, or whatever, arrive there knowing that you gave your all, your best.

God gives you an intellect for a reason. God wouldn't have given it to us if he just wanted us to believe on faith. God could have snapped his fingers and said, "You've all got to believe in me now." It's our God-given duty to search for him through logic, through science, through reasoning, through common sense.

Science and Faith

I have science and logic to back up my religious beliefs, rather than just faith. Science is a passion of mine. What sense does it make for science to contradict religion? If you ask someone if they believe in God and they say yes, they'll have to admit that God was the creator of everything. Therefore, God had to be the creator of gravity. He had to be the creator of the sun, the moon, and the stars. All the laws of physics—he's the one who created them. Why would God say one thing with his works and creation and then do another with his religion?

In Islam, there are no contradictions between science and religion. The Qur'an—you can read it backwards, forwards, inside out, upside down, whatever—you're not going to find a contradiction between religion and science. What you will find is that science supports the Qur'an.

When my dad first encouraged me to study other religions, I was thinking, "Why is he encouraging me? Doesn't he want me to be Muslim?" And now it occurred to me that of course he wanted me to be Muslim. Now I understand what it means to be a Muslim.

The Qur'an Is What Saved Me

Kamran, 21
Muslim

When I was fourteen or fifteen, my parents got divorced. There was a personal crisis in my life. I started to question and doubt everything I took for granted, like, "Is there really a God out there?" "I've always tried to live a good life and not hurt anyone—why is God doing this to me?" "Isn't God supposed to be merciful?" They are questions which any person of religion goes through at one point in their lives.

I had just finished reading the Qur'an. After eighth grade, I took a year off and I had a sabbatical. I memorized the Qur'an in Arabic. It took me nine months. I've recommended it to a lot of people. My memory increased significantly. I developed a way of learning and being able to take in huge chunks of information and recall them. It helped me to develop a system of personal discipline. I found spiritual tranquility from that.

Joseph

When I was experiencing my personal crisis, the Qur'an is what saved me. That's where I found solace. Then the most meaningful chapter in the Qur'an was the story of the prophet Joseph. According to the Qur'an, Joseph was the son of the great prophet Jacob. His stepbrothers were extremely jealous of him, because Jacob loved Joseph and his blood brother, Benjamin, the most. They plotted with each other to get rid of Joseph by throwing him into a well and telling their father that a wolf had eaten him. Joseph was rescued from the well by a caravan who sold him into slavery, and he ended up becoming the slave of the minister of the Pharaoh in Egypt.

Joseph was also an extremely beautiful human being. When he reaches adulthood, the wife of the minister seeks to seduce him. He resists. They put him in prison. Later, Pharaoh has a dream that none of the courtiers and ministers can interpret. A prison mate of Joseph remembers Joseph's talent for interpreting dreams and tells the king. Joseph correctly interprets the dream, and the king is impressed and wants to make him a minister. Joseph insists that the woman who sought to imprison him be brought forth and his innocence declared. He then is put in charge of the treasury and grain distribution for the upcoming famine.

Years later, at the peak of the famine, his brothers come for grain. Joseph recognizes them, but they don't recognize him. He tells them to return with Benjamin the next time. On their next visit, Joseph tells one of his servants to hide the precious drinking cup of the king in the bag of Benjamin. As the brothers are departing, a crier cries out that the cup has been stolen. Joseph then orders the party to be searched, and when the cup is found in Benjamin's bag, Benjamin is forced to stay behind.

By now, Jacob has gone blind from crying out of despair for his beloved son. Hearing about the loss of Benjamin drives him to even more sorrow, but he tells his sons, "Never despair of the mercy of God. Indeed, only the disbelievers despair of the mercy of God." This was something that certainly rang in my ears during my difficult times. Eventually, the brothers return to Joseph again for grain. In a moment of triumph, Joseph reveals who he is, and his brothers fall before him for forgiveness. But Joseph forgives them for their transgressions.

When I read what Joseph had to go through—being tortured, and thrown into jail, and all these other things—his struggle and eventual triumph spoke to me. He never lost his faith and trust in the Divine. That chapter had a significant influence on my life.

There is a verse in the Qur'an, "Does mankind reckon that because they say, 'we believe,' that they shall be left alone and not be given trials and tribulations?" I realized that everything is a test from God and his way is to test those who are the closest to him. Perhaps my test was an indication that God wanted me to be close to him through my patience and maintenance of my faith.

I feel that I learned some significant lifelong lessons from this period of doubt. In the end, I came back full circle to where I started. And if anything, that period of questioning and doubt strengthened my faith and my resolve as to what role my religion plays in my life. And that spiritual foundation helps me to carry out whatever tasks I set out to do.

I Thought That God Was Just Nonexistent

Esther,* 19
Christian
*not her real name

I grew up in a Christian home. My dad was a pastor. My parents were married for twenty years, and about eighteen of those twenty years my dad cheated on my mom. When I was eight years old, I found this out.

We were told that we had to keep it a secret or else my dad could lose his job. I pretty much grew up going to church every Sunday, watching my dad, who was cheating on my mom, tell me that it was wrong to do that. And I thought that God was just nonexistent. But I couldn't say anything about it 'cause my dad was so overpowering, so overbearing.

When I was sixteen, my mom finally said she wanted a divorce. The church found out what he had been doing, and he got fired from his job. At that time, I told him that I didn't want to see him anymore. Then I stopped going to church completely and started to get into everything that a sixteen-year-old can get into. I started drinking and became addicted very quickly.

About a year-and-a-half later, I met up with some friends who were Christians. They went to a local youth group, so I started going with them. Everything I heard I had already heard before because I'd grown up in a house where the Bible was thrown down your throat. So I knew all the stories. But I didn't understand.

So my junior year, I went away on a retreat, and I listened to this speaker talk about having a personal relationship with Jesus Christ. He said if there was any relationship in your life that was hindering you from growing closer to God, you should talk to somebody. Immediately, I knew that my father was. So I went and talked to somebody and told her about my dad and how much I hated him—how much I hated church and God. And she asked me, "How do you know that you're going to go to heaven?"

I said, "Well, because I believe in Jesus." That was what you were supposed to say. She said, "You believe in him, but do you trust in him?" And it occurred to me that if Jesus did die for my sins, then I needed to trust him and believe that he did do that and that I was forgiven for everything I had done. So at that moment, I started to believe in that, trust in that.

And about four months later, I was able to go and talk to my dad. I realized that even though he had done all those things, I still had to forgive him. So I did. Now, about three years later, I talk to him on a regular basis. I love him as my father.

If you have questions and doubts about faith, what can you do? Many of the people I interviewed turned to others for guidance with mixed results. For example, one young man who is a member of a Christian orthodox church said: "As far as our religion is concerned, you're not supposed to question God's actions. You're not supposed to question life. It just is. Sometimes you feel like, 'Is there really a God?' But that's a sin."

Some people and religious groups do not promote much independent thinking, says James Fowler. Fowler's advice: "Take yourself seriously and take the options or the challenges life presents you seriously. Find people who have integrity and make the time and find the courage to talk with them about the things that matter most to you." Look for people who are willing to be vulnerable and share their struggles and their journey with you.

Also, Fowler adds, young people can look for faith communities—a house of worship, a youth group, for example—that "encourage you to be in a growth mode with your faith and provide both contexts and experiences that stimulates growth and reflection." These groups, says Fowler, "challenge you to look at the faith tradition and practices in a deeper way, but also give you permission to be in tension with it."

The doubts of some people I spoke to are not easily resolved. For them, faith and doubt coexist. Others resolved their doubts by leaving religion.

I Can Appreciate My Degree of Uncertainty

Sean, 20
Christian (Catholic)

I was raised Catholic in a sort of way. Every once in a while we'd go to church—an average of once a month. The more younger siblings I had, the less often we'd be able to go because little kids in those big rooms—they'll start crying or something, and it just echoes, and it's embarrassing. Now I go when somebody either gets married or dies.

I don't think kids really like going to church. You have to put on your nice clothes, and you have to sit still and be quiet for an hour. It's not generally a fun thing. So when you're little, you're going because your parents are telling you to go. And when they stop telling you to go, you're not going to just get up and head over there. I don't think it's necessarily a bad thing that I don't go around practicing religion. I think it's left me a little bit more open to finding out what I believe rather than be told what I believe.

I have trouble understanding people who are really strong in their faith. It seems like it would be a lot of energy and a lot of work. I can kind of admire it in people and kind of envy that they feel so comfortable and confident in their beliefs.

Here in America, you can have all the religion you want, but it better stay in your house and your church—and maybe something on your car bumper or key chain. We're not allowed to practice religion really loudly and openly because we're at risk of offending eight to ten other types of people who could be nearby. You put up a nativity scene in a public area, you're going to get sued.

We're a country that tries to focus on what we have in common rather than what we have different. If you don't talk about it and you don't look at it, then eventually you just don't think about it anymore. And then after a while, you're not going to believe it anymore, either.

In high school, there were some kids. They'd go out and meet by the flag-pole and have their own little personal prayer sessions. There would be a group of maybe twenty or thirty Christians who would get together.

There were other people who would walk by in the morning and go, "Those Jesus freaks really piss me off." People start to feel threatened when somebody says, "I'm living my life the way God wants me to." They have a sense of superiority about them, like: "We're strong in our faith, and we're going to heaven, and we're better than you because of this." It's just kind of a vibe you get. It might not even be a vibe they're giving off as much as you start to feel it.

But I think there's a point where there's a closed-mindedness involved. I don't feel like I'd have to understand more to be with them. It's almost like I'd have to be dumber or more gullible to fall in with that crowd. They wake up in the morning and go, "Well, I went to church last Sunday, so I'm a good person." I'm left to analyzing my behavior and stuff like that.

Some use their religion in lieu of developing a moral code. They feel that since a requirement for being a good person is doing these things, they don't have to worry about these other things.

I suppose in a way I'd feel sort of inferior to somebody like that because they're so confident that the way they're living their life is right. But I can appreciate my degree of uncertainty.

People write of Jesus as a teacher—not as somebody who believed in blind faith. They always talk about him sitting under a tree surrounded by his followers. And he would talk to them about things, and they would gradually intellectually come around to his way of thinking. I think if you believe in something on an intellectual level, it's a much stronger belief and much more adaptable to situations than if you believe in something as a knee-jerk reflex because that was how you were brought up.

Useful Lies

I think people have kind of gotten themselves into a group of metaphors that works for them. Have you ever read *Cat's Cradle*? It's a Kurt Vonnegut book. The leader of this religion tells his followers, "This religion isn't real." He says it's based entirely on something he calls "useful lies." These are lies that make you feel better, make you live your life better, so it's OK to treat them as truth.

I think that a lot of religions have a system of useful lies. They help people live their lives in a more moral sort of way. They go to church and they get a sense of community if they hang around with a lot of people who share similar beliefs. At the end of the day, they feel better about themselves. So it was useful for them.

It's frustrating, because with a lot of subjects, I feel that once I'm done talking about it, I've come to a real understanding. And all I ever seem to get when I think and talk about religion is a headache and a dry mouth. It's kind of baffling for somebody like me, who is generally able to figure other things out.

I Believe in Something

I suppose I have to believe in something, just because there's so much complexity in the universe that I don't think it could all have been completely random.

Like I don't believe in creationism, just because Christianity believes that God said, "Let there be light!" and all of a sudden the universe was there. I think evolution, Darwinism—all that happened. What people should realize is that, if there is a God, he'd be clever enough to coordinate something on such a large scale that it would take thousands of our scientists to even figure out a part of it. I don't think he'd be so uninspired as to just kind of flip a light switch and the universe would be there. I believe that God set up a lot of things in advance. He set up the laws of nature to work the way they work. He put the moon here, he put the stars over there, and then he put a bunch of people there and gave them free will to do whatever they were inclined to do.

I don't think God snaps his fingers and makes an earthquake erupt out of the ground—that's tectonic plates hitting each other. **If somebody gets eaten by a bear in the woods, it's not because God was mad. It's because they were walking through the woods with bacon in their backpack.**

When a bad person takes power and kills a bunch of other people, some people think, "How could God let that happen?" I think it's a way of not taking responsibility. Well, how did we let that happen?

I think there are definitely abuses that a church can hand out to people. But they do bring communities together. They set up organizations for battered wives and homeless people. There are priests working in soup kitchens. And I think there are a lot of people in these organizations that have a desire to do good.

A couple thousand years ago, religion was essential in establishing a civilized society, spreading reading and writing, and transcribing historical events, and just creating a general hierarchy that we needed to accomplish more than just isolated tribes ever could. I think religion served a major purpose then.

My Grandfather's Faith

I think my grandfather was really helped by his faith. He died a couple years ago. When I went to his funeral, there were a lot of people there just because they knew him from church. They knew the tall guy that sat in the back and who would write letters to the priest and get into little debates. There was an entire row of people who used to sit with him, and they were there because they were gonna miss him. I think it brought him a good deal of comfort to know that he was part of something.

I like to have a history with something even if I don't practice it now. It's kind of nice to know that my family comes from this belief system.

This God Didn't Make Any Sense

Kara, 23
Atheist

I had been baptized as a Catholic, but I never made my first communion. My parents weren't really committed to religion. There were just kind of vague ideas of God. Like when I asked where babies come from, the answer was, "Well, Mommy and Daddy pray to God, and he gives them a baby." Growing up, I went to church maybe three times.

I went to a public school. Back in fifth and sixth grades, I remember having questions about the separation of church and state. Like I had questions about the Pledge of Allegiance. I don't know where they came from exactly. Maybe I was learning about the Constitution in class and started to say, "I am seeing God at school." There was a teacher who wanted to put this little chick I made in home ec class, a stuffed animal, in this Easter display. I absolutely rejected that and tried to get rid of the Easter display. I didn't know if I believed in God or not, but either way I knew it shouldn't be in the school.

In high school I had serious questions about God. I kind of went back and forth. There were times when I seriously believed in God and I was going to Young Life, a young Christian group where they sang songs and chanted and stuff like that. But eventually I just started to get more critical in my thinking, like, "If there is a God that will have an impact on things, I should try to figure this out."

I took classes about the Bible, and it just seemed like a total myth to me. This God didn't make any sense and didn't have the rationality that I would expect a God to have. There is a huge amount of injustice in the world—poverty, exploitation—that happens to people who do not deserve it, while others live in luxury and do not deserve it. **A rational God would stop this craziness.**

It wasn't such a struggle for me to give up the idea of God and become an atheist. It was just affirming what I might have always thought anyway. I think we're immersed in a society that's pushing the idea of God in all these various and vague ways. But to me, I don't see any proof. I had this disbelief in spirituality or the existence of anything beyond the material world and consciousness. No one was ever able to show me that spirituality existed. So I just accepted that there was no God. I didn't call myself an atheist. It was just a side note.

One Nation Under . . .

I haven't gotten a huge reaction from anyone. My parents found out I was an atheist when we were riding in the car on the way back from my grandma's house. On the radio, they were talking about the issue of the Pledge of Allegiance in schools and whether or not God should be included in it—"one nation under God." And I was like, "That so obviously should be taken out."

But my parents were going, "No, why? If people are atheists, that's fine. They don't have to say that part. But the rest of us believe in God, and so it should be included." And I was like, "No, I think that's ridiculous."

They're like, "Don't you believe in God?" I'm like, "Well, no." There was a little pause. I think it scares my mom a little bit. She has these vague ideas that I might go to hell. It was just smoothed over and not talked about.

I guess in the last year, I started to affirm the fact that, "Hey, I am an atheist, and this does mean something." It's really been a big part of my life. I had this teacher last fall, and his class was this huge challenge to me. It was a regular speech class. But the way he taught it was like mass group discussion, and every once in a while, you had to get up and talk. So we started with these really controversial topics. The first topic we talked about was the [Iraq] war.

A lot of people were basing these prowar positions and other various political positions on God. Islamic extremists put God on their side. But I was seeing it on our side as well. George Bush and other federal officials put God rhetoric into their speeches. And kids in the class, like the seriously religious people, were like, "We believe that things are the way they are for a reason. And they should stay that way and allow for God's hand to guide us through everything."

You Can't Count on God to Step In.

For me it was like, "You can't count on a God to step in." It's up to humans to decide what the future will be. And so the fact that I was an atheist makes me more proactive because I don't have any hope for a life beyond life or any sort of supernatural experience. So I have this real sense of urgency in my life—this is all the time that you have; you better do something with it.

The Pledge of Allegiance is a kind of sick thing—like I'm pledging allegiance and I'm pledging subservience. I think the idea of God goes back to that a lot—a belief that somebody knows what's better for you. You're pledging allegiance to your country and your God. And that's taking a very submissive role, which I won't accept.

Religion has been used as a defense for slavery and other horribly oppressive relations. Throughout history people have allowed horrible conditions to go on without changing them because they believed "the meek shall inherit the Earth" or that if they're modest in this life and accept things the way they are, something is promised to them after this. They're not basing things on what really is, what really could be, and what their potential could be.

It's like the working class all over the world just accepting things the way they are. It happens here in the United States. Like in a lot of the South Side [of Chicago] are these totally impoverished people who accept things. A lot of businesses are totally run-down. What you see replacing these businesses are these churches. It's a real symbol to me. To me, that's not what's going to emancipate them. It's not going to raise people out of those conditions all over the world. It's something that just reinforces what's going on.

You don't have to have God to be a moral person. People think that without God there's chaos. But I think there is an order to things, that people are not inherently selfish, that they can be molded to a number of different things. **A disbelief in God can be a belief in human beings and faith in their ability to make life worthwhile on this planet for what we really do have, as opposed to what might be made up for us.**

In recent years, scientific and technological breakthroughs have created new challenges to religious beliefs, especially beliefs about the creation and sanctity of human life. Doctors now create human embryos in test tubes. Geneticists have recently decoded the human genome, the material that is the blueprint for human life. Some scientists claim to be attempting to clone a human being.

The conflict between science and religion is nothing new. An example is the ongoing battle between Americans who argue that life on Earth began in the Garden of Eden, as written in Genesis, and those who support the theory that life on Earth evolved over millions of years. Today, the creationism/evolution controversy is being played out in classrooms around the country as parents and educators on both sides feud over the content of curricula and textbooks.

How do young people deal with conflicts between faith and science? Anthony was someone who wrestled with this the most.

A Cup of Wine and a Piece of Bread Can Then Become God

Anthony, 23
Christian (Catholic)

I have degrees in computer science and physics. For me, science is how I find my religious justifications for things. And then I see how they fit into Catholicism.

At our mass, at the period of consecration, the idea is that the bread and wine physically become Jesus, and then we take that. For some people, it's a definite struggling point. It was for me, until I studied physics in high school and college.

The biggest revelation for me was in thermal physics class in college. The teacher walked into the classroom and said, "This is the hardest concept you will ever learn in your entire life." He drew a box on the board. He put a dot in it. He said, "What's the possibility that this dot is in the box?" Everyone's like, "One-hundred percent, right?"

He says, "No, there are no 100 percents in the universe. Something may be highly improbable, but everything is possible. It's always going to be 99.9, with a billion 9s after it, that this dot is in the box. But there's that five-billion 0.1 that this dot's on Mars. And that's a quantum idea.

"So anything that can happen will happen—it's only a matter of time and space. It might take 10,000 or 10 million years before it comes true. To accept the quantum idea, you must accept the fact that there's no 100 percent and there's no 0 percent, only things in between probability and improbability."

I always saw God as the universe. Quantum physics gave me more concrete terms to put things in that I had always felt. I think that God doesn't directly interfere with creation—he sets up the rules and exists but doesn't come in and meddle unless something calls on him for help.

For me, it would make sense that a cup of wine and a piece of bread can then become God. But I don't think the priests themselves have the power to do this, I think the congregation does. I feel that a group of people can call upon God to become physically present. God the universe then becomes more concentrated in the body and blood of this wine and bread. It becomes more concentrated as those people call upon it.

And then you take this inspiration, this divineness, into yourself. If I'm at mass and I'm not present mentally, then that transubstantiation is not going to happen for me, but it might happen for people next to me.[26]

Different Paths to the Same Place

That quantum idea got me to thinking—maybe logical choice isn't always the right choice. Maybe emotion, and trusting your conscience and what you feel, does have a place. It got me to merge my two worlds, allowed that spirituality and science to coexist at the same time.

In many parts of the world, people inherit the faith of their parents. The idea of choice in religion is very American, says R. Stephen Warner, a professor of sociology at the University of Illinois at Chicago and director of the Youth and Religion Project. Says Warner:

> *America is very different religiously. There are people who grow up in very encapsulated communities, but they are few. Most people grow up knowing that there is somebody else out there, there are other ways of being. So to just say, "I'm Catholic because my dad is" doesn't cut it. We have to own who we are—that's part of American culture and has been for a very long time.*
>
> *Reinventing yourself, making yourself over, is deeply American. That's not to say that everybody gives it a lot of thought. But you'll run into people making themselves over in different directions: "I grope with religion, I reject religion." "I grew up with this religion and I embrace that religion." "I grew up with no religion, and I embrace religion."*

---

[26] Transubstantiation is the Catholic doctrine that during the Eucharist the bread and wine are transformed into the body and blood of Jesus, without altering its appearance.

More than 33 million people—about 16 percent of the 18-and-older population in the U.S.—have changed their religious identification during their lifetime, according to estimates from the American Religious Identification Survey 2001. For many of these people, changing religious identification meant leaving religion. The number of American adults who do not identify with a religion doubled from 1990 to 2001, according to the survey. In 2001 an estimated 14.1 percent of U.S. adults did not identify with a religion.

The estimated share of people who have changed their religious identification "significantly understates the amount of in-and-out movement from religious communities that we have," says Warner. "It doesn't take into account the millions of people who don't change their religious identities but go way down and up in the importance that their religion has for them. Most people go through these phases."

For many people, the decision to switch from one faith to another involves months or years of study, soul searching, and spiritual reflection. It often involves loss—something is given up.

Patrick, a former Christian, describes his journey to Buddhism.

If You Don't Like Something, You Don't Have to Accept It

Patrick, 19
Buddhist, former Christian

I went to a nondenominational Christian church in Round Lake until I was about seventeen. I started going with my best friend and his family.

My father wasn't always there. And so my parents got divorced and then he moved to Florida. I think I was like six or seven. We kept in touch. And then it got more infrequent and then, eventually, at this point, it's just like maybe a birthday card or a call on occasion.

I guess you look for what you need in your life, and God is what you need him to be. And in my life, God was a father figure. I was kind of afraid of him, but they teach that you're supposed to fear God. He is all-powerful. He has the control to do the best things in your life and the control to make things horrible for you.

For a long time—for five, six years—Christianity did it for me. I would go to church, and when I would come home I'd have a positive feeling inside of me, like I'm a good person and I'm making the best of my life. But then it just wasn't enough. It just wasn't working.

I stopped going to church. I started reading on my own because the whole idea of organized religions started turning me off. One of my good friends is a Zen Buddhist. I asked her about it. She gave me a couple books at the library to check out. I read up on Buddhism, and it really appealed to me.

Since I moved, I've got completely new friends. It allowed me to reevaluate my life and pursue different things, which is part of why I stopped attending church and I converted to Buddhism.

Living the Best Life

The branch of Buddhism that I found is like Zen Buddhism, but much less strict. It's an Americanized form of Buddhism. I am probably not a very good Buddhist. I don't meditate every day. I'm not a vegan, though I tried for two months. But in just the basic principles, I do a pretty good job of integrating them into my daily routine.

What's important to Buddhists, at least the way I interpret it, is you live a good life, be mindful of what you're doing, and attain enlightenment, or *zazen*, a state of nirvana. You can attain zazen through meditation, or whatever does it for you. If you don't like something, you don't have to accept it. The only thing that matters is your pursuit of life. If you want to be both Buddhist and Christian, that's fine. Whatever works is what's right for you.

If you just look at Christianity, there are a lot of references and stories that could help people with their lives. It gave me a purpose—not like, "I'm going to preach the word." But like, "I can live the best life that I can live for God." And now, it's more like, "I can live my life the best that I can live for me." It's a really small word difference, but it's a huge, huge difference.

I think that God is omniscient and he's in everything. I can't say that I don't believe in a higher force, because there's just things that I can't explain and that are too beautiful to just be random occurrences from chaos. But, you know, I'm not going to worry about that.

My Own God

Buddhism doesn't recognize or refute the existence of God, because that's technically not important to them. I feel that to a certain extent, I am my own God—not that I am a god or anything, but that I have control over certain things. My life is ultimately to be lived by me. I feel that I have a purpose in life, and I'm going to pursue that for me.

Darcy was once ambivalent about her faith. But her chosen path was not conversion to another religion or to a secular life. She thinks that some young people are too quick to give up their faith.

Consider Sticking with What You Have

Darcy, 23
Jewish (Modern Orthodox)

College was probably the time when I was the most unreligious of my life simply because there was no community. I'm Orthodox. I don't like praying in non-Orthodox synagogues. If you don't have positive reinforcement, it's very hard to stay religious and keep doing everything you should be doing as a Jew. I admit I slipped a little bit. Then I decided that if I went on like this, I wouldn't be Jewish at all, and I got my act back together. I went and stayed with Jewish families on the North Side for *Shabbos* or went to Hillel. But it was really hard.

Asking G-d

Whenever I have problems or question my religion, I just ask G-d directly what I should be doing. A rabbi is not an intermediary between you and G-d. He's simply someone who has studied the laws and can clarify them for you. If you have a problem with G-d, you talk to G-d about it. If you want to register a complaint or a request or say thank you for something, you talk to G-d yourself. And you can do it any way you want—you can make up a prayer in your head, you can say it out loud, you can go to services and say something to yourself.

Religion and Identity

When you're a teenager, young adult, it's very natural to start questioning your religion because you're questioning your identity and who you are and where you are and how you fit into the world. But if I had to make a recommendation, it would be: Feel free to do some exploring. But consider sticking with what you have until you figure out your identity, and then your religion makes much more sense.

So I would suggest that if you're going to change your religion, wait until you're more settled in life, like early twenties, or when you at least have some idea of who you are. Then see if you're really dissatisfied with your religion, or you're just dissatisfied with other things and you're just attributing it to religion.

This comes out of my personal experience. When I start straying a bit far off the road, sometimes all it takes is hearing a particular phrase—the *Kaddish* or the *Sh'ma*—to remind me of everything—who I am, what I am, where I belong. Every religious Jew who has been to synagogue immediately recognizes the Kaddish. It basically says, "Blessed and sanctified be G-d's name," and it goes on in the same vein. When they become not religious and they hear it, it always reminds them of who they are and what they came from. I think it would be really sad if you lose that at the time when you need it most, if you lose your foundation when you need it most.

Watered-down wine is not very good, neither is watered-down religion. Many parents choose to be less religious in an attempt to make their children happier by avoiding all the strictures and limitations Orthodoxy places upon them. These well-intentioned people do not realize that you cannot pick and choose in religion and come up with any meaningful cohesive whole.

My religion makes sense to me because I know what the rules are and what they mean, even if I personally choose not to follow some of them. But you cannot cut out half of Judaism, make it meaningless, and expect your children to understand and appreciate it.

How Can I Know God Better?

Savva's faith journey is guided by the question "How can I know God better?" When we spoke, Savva, who was born a Jew, was considering conversion to a new faith. That decision, he realizes, may have a high price.

Savva, 20
Jewish

I was born in Moscow, Russia. I left when I was seven. I've been living here for the past thirteen years.

Just a little bit of history—some Russians can be Jewish, but you couldn't be a practicing Jew in Russia. When I was growing up in Russia, you weren't allowed to practice religion of any kind. This was true for everyone, not only Jews. It was very bad if you got caught going to synagogue. It was dangerous. Because of that, my parents never raised me to be religious, and their parents never raised them to be religious. I guess the Communist Party was the one and only thing that you could pledge allegiance to.

On the other hand, the fact that I was Jewish was written in my passport, and we got discriminated against because we were Jewish. There were certain jobs that Jews didn't get. They just saw "Jewish" written on the passport, and a job was denied to them, or they couldn't get into a certain university. So it was kind of that Catch-22 where an identity is forced on you, but you really can't live out that identity.

My grandfather was very exceptional, both because of the position he held and because he managed to practice in secrecy. He had a very high-ranking job in the government. He had a lot of clout, and it was very surprising because he was Jewish. But he also would secretly go to synagogue. He was caught once for it and almost lost his job. And now that he's in America, he goes to synagogue every Saturday morning. He started practicing more and more, and he reads the Torah on a weekly basis.

It's kind of evident in my parents' attitude toward religion now—attachment to Judaism and repulsion from organized religion. On one hand, it's been driven into them that they're Jewish. They have a very strong attachment to being Jewish, but it's very cultural. If you ask them many questions about what Judaism is, they don't know because they were never brought up with it.

Religious School

Right after I came here I was in an American school. I didn't know the language or anything. Then I went to a transitional school for a little while. I was around ten when my parents sent me to a Jewish school for two years. It was Orthodox, which for a nonpracticing Jew was quite a shock. Imagine me—knowing no English, no Hebrew, and no Jewish customs—and thrust into an Orthodox Jewish-American school. It was pretty horrible for a kid my age, especially because kids are mean. They'd make fun of my accent. I just didn't fit in. I didn't know anything—from what the Torah was to how to play baseball.

And very early on, I very quickly developed a pretty bad taste for organized religion because it was 1) forced on me, 2) completely unknown to me, and 3) the kids were really mean. I thought, "I'm Jewish, they're Jewish, but look how mean they are to me."

From day one, I had to start praying, because there's prayer in the morning and during the day. And I had to start learning the Torah and Hebrew and all these things, and it was very difficult. I had a hard time keeping up or fitting in. I did everything by rote, knowing very little about the meaning behind what I was studying. Then, by sixth grade, I left the Orthodox school and started going to Old Orchard, a regular junior high school.

And even though I left the Orthodox school, what stuck with me was this idea that I had to pray. It was semi-fear or something, but I kept praying. I would pray in the morning and night and before eating and stuff.

Basically my Hebrew deteriorated, so I started saying my prayers in English. **And I would just start saying in English what I thought I should have been saying in Hebrew, and as that happened more and more, and as I began to shape the meaning behind the words of my prayers, I felt like my prayers were being answered.** It was through a very natural, very gradual transformation from a forced, noninvolved prayer life to a very involved, very personal, daily prayer life that I saw changes—a connection was forming. I didn't feel like I was talking to myself or saying things into thin air.

MY FAITH JOURNEY

"I'm Not Religious, I'm Spiritual."

Now that I think back on it, it was kind of miraculous, like the greatest experience in my life stretched out over time. And I began to say that I'm not religious, I'm spiritual, because I didn't really have a religion per se. Many people around me were religious, but I wasn't quite sure how spiritual they were. They kind of did the rote thing.

I decided that I wanted to go back into religion—on my own terms, at my own speed, and reexplore my Judaism. So I went on a trip to Israel right after high school. It was a very religious, explore-the-roots-of-Judaism sort of trip, and it was great. And after that, I went to college. We have a great, active Hillel, and I joined the Hillel, and I started going to services there. I started getting involved in Jewish life on campus in all sorts of ways, and it was great. I felt like I was combining my spirituality with my Judaism, and I was doing it at my own pace. For a long time, I was just studying Judaism and really getting into that. I was challenging myself, learning, and kept getting in more depth.

And then I met my best friend freshman year. He is Baha'i, and we began to have these conversations. And I began thinking of whether or not there are common strands and connections between faiths—that's what the Baha'i faith believes. These ideas of interconnectedness in faiths and relationships between faiths really began to bother me. I couldn't just brush them off. Being true to my intellect, I had to address them: Why are there different faiths? Why am I Jewish? Am I Jewish just 'cause I happened to be born into it? Or am I Jewish because it's my choice 100 percent to accept this faith?

And after about half a year's worth of conversations, rather than just studying Judaism, I decided to study other faiths, just to prove them right or wrong. I was doing a Jewish study group. I was studying the Bible with a Christian partner. I met with a Muslim partner at the end of this year, and we're going to be meeting next year. And I was studying the Baha'i faith. I'm helping to found a Jewish-Muslim dialogue group on the Middle East. I'm also taking intergroup dialogue classes.

Questioning the Very Essence of Who I Am

So I started studying other faiths and getting introduced to a lot of different ideas. And I really began questioning the very essence of who I am and why I am what I am. So right now, after what's probably been two years of studying, a lot of different interactions, and a lot of different conversations with people,

I'm very much at a point where I'm leaning more toward the Baha'i faith. After all of that exploration, I feel like I've seen an overwhelming amount of connectedness between faiths. And the Baha'i premise—that there is one God, and all faiths come from that one God, and all faiths are connected, and there is a bigger spiritual truth—I am leaning toward very strongly. So that's why I say I'm considering converting.

There's a lot of exploration and a lot of prayer and a lot of spiritual energy that I've devoted to this. When I come to my grandparents and I ask them why I shouldn't do this, they really can't give me a spiritual answer because they haven't read the Torah, they haven't studied. They just have a very deeply entrenched feeling of "You should be Jewish."

I've always said to them that I will be Jewish culturally. It can be very beautiful to be culturally Jewish in terms of food, ritual, and family. But there is another part to what it means to being born Jewish. I know that if there were another Holocaust, I would be killed because it wouldn't matter what I believed spiritually. It means in the end, a label is put on you.

I believe Judaism is a God-given tradition and that the Torah is a God-sent writing. Beyond that, it becomes very difficult. But am I spiritually and religiously Jewish? It's the question I've asked of myself because I want to know why it is that I follow this religion. Is it that I should keep the Sabbath—is that what God wants? Or to keep kosher—is that what God asks of me? And when I ask those questions, I get confused because there are so many ways of being religiously Jewish—all the way from Ultra Orthodox to Ultra Liberal and Reform. And all those people will say they're Jewish, except they do completely different things in many cases. Some will keep kosher and say they're Jewish, and some won't. Some will keep a certain level of it, and some won't. Some will celebrate, and some won't. And that bothers me.

The thing that I'm most scared about is that I'm incredibly entrenched in the Jewish community—friendships, the roles that I hold, and the positions. By all those standards, I'm very, very Jewish.

On the other hand, I always want to stay true to myself and always want to keep challenging myself. I can feel when I'm challenged and growing spiritually—it's a very exciting, energizing feeling. And what's very scary is that it's more and more seeming like becoming Baha'i or converting is the next step for me.

MY FAITH JOURNEY

Who I Am, How Others See Me

To me, identity has two elements to it. One is who I think I am, and that is fluid and something that I can rethink on a daily basis. I can add on to myself. It's important to stay true to myself and not to pretend. But external identity—that which is imposed on you by others and what others think you are—is a very hard thing to negotiate and very difficult to get a grasp on and shape. And so it will be a shock to some people if I convert, and socially it would just be a mess. Even though I might think I'm the same person—only spiritually advanced or spiritually growing—other people would in no way look at me like that.

The one thing that I could always come back to is my spiritual life because that's always stayed true to me. I became spiritually minded first, before being religiously minded. **For me, the question isn't "Which religion am I?" It's more like, "How can I know God better?"**

And at the end of the day, when I'm afraid or unsure, it always comes down to a belief in God and daily prayer. And in daily prayer I feel a lot of acceptance and understanding and encouragement and guidance. Having that relationship and feeling like God gently guides me along to where I should be is very comforting. I feel like I'm being guided toward correct decisions.

I've talked to a lot of people about their faith and why they are who they are. I've heard a lot of religious stories. And the saddest to me is when the person does what they do and they don't even know why. They're not even sure how God fits into the picture.

Some of the happiest stories for me are when the person begins their journey and their discussion starting with God. Those are the people, I've noticed, who are open to interfaith and different ways of doing things. I feel they're more confident because they have something more solid that they're resting on. They can question and look around because they're perched on such a solid foundation.

I think it comes down to where a person is grounded. Where I'm grounded is faith in God.

Strength, Meaning, Hope

In an ongoing four-year study, researchers at the University of North Carolina at Chapel Hill are examining the religious practices of thousands of youths across the country. Christian Smith, professor and associate chair of sociology at the university, is the director of the National Study of Youth and Religion. Says Professor Smith:

Innumerable studies have clearly shown that the more religiously active U.S. teens and their families are, the more those teens avoid risky and unhealthy behaviors, participate in constructive social activities, and have stronger family relationships. There is a definite, positive, empirical association between teen religious involvement and more positive, constructive outcomes in teens' lives.

This book is filled with dozens of testimonials about the power of religion in young people's lives. On the following pages you'll read some compelling stories about how faith carried people through especially trying times, as well as the trials of everyday life.

I Knew That I Might Not Wake Up

Evan, 21
Christian (Evangelical)

When I was in kindergarten, I was diagnosed with epilepsy. About that time, my folks had gone through a divorce, and I was suffering through some very difficult ordeals. And about that same time—I was about seven years old—I came to know Christ as my savior, as my God. If I hadn't known Christ personally, I wouldn't be alive today.

I have been close to passing away about four times, and I have had a number of real painful years of health problems. I had to have brain surgery and many other operations, and I have had a lot of internal-organ disorders.

When I had the brain surgery, it was still very experimental, and I was a test case. They videotaped it and showed it at universities. I was fourteen years old. The chances of me surviving the surgery were not very promising. My folks were really distraught about it because the surgeon was removing my right temporal lobe. But I never once worried about it. I had incredible peace, especially lying in my hospital bed. I was in God's presence. **If I hadn't known Christ, there is no way, no way at all, that I would have had the perseverance or the endurance to push on.**

I was talking to a neurologist last August, and I told him I was attending college. He said that that is a miracle, because nearly one percent of the one percent who have epilepsy and have had brain surgery finishes high school. After the amount of brain they took out of my head, most people are vegetables for the rest of their lives. And he said, "That's just a testimony of something good in your life." It's an allusion to God's great work.

Without Jesus Christ in my life, I am afraid to know where I'd be today. He has saved my life many times over. There were times when I stared death in the face and I knew that I might not wake up. But in the midst of the storms, I had intense peace and immense joy and I could fall asleep knowing that I'd be going to be with my Savior. There was nothing that was going to shake my faith.

I have seen the glory of God the most in my suffering. God loves me so much that he has caused me to suffer so that his grace would sustain me in order to make his glory known. He has educated me most through the fires of suffering and the school of tears.

A life crisis—a death, a divorce, an illness, for example—can trigger a crisis of faith. People suffering loss often ask why a loving, just God would send pain and suffering their way.

An experience of tragedy or loss can drive someone away from his or her faith. But these experiences can also cause people to go deeper into their faith, where they find solace, support, and most important, meaning in their loss.

Torrence wrote this rap after he learned that his brother had died. He took part in Project A.S.T.R.O. (Art Studies toward Real Opportunities), a not-for-profit organization that provides free arts instruction for foster youth.

Still My Dawg

Torrence, 18 (15 when written)
Christian (Baptist)

Hey Tommy, Datch, Paul, Mama.
I don't know about y'all, but I can't deal with this drama.
Everybody leaving right to left.
I don't know 'bout them, but I ain't ready to meet death.

Look what's left—just me and the family.
People coming after me, trying to splatter me.
Mama always told me that I had a hard head
and that if I didn't listen now I would surely be dead.

I went up the ladder and said it's 'bout to begin.
I fell, went back up, and I came down again.
Lord forgive me for my sins. I don't mean to be bad,
but you keep taking people out of my life. You leaving me sad.

People always telling me, "Torrence, things happen for a reason
this time of the year—this part of the season."
People steady dying. What's the reason for that—
Shawn, Tommy, Mama, Paul, and then it was Datch.

I got leeches on my back, and they sucking my blood.
When stuff like this happens, it makes me wanna get a gun,
go kill everybody who ever brought me trouble.
I'm picturing it in my mind, taking my life on the double.

I'm getting the shovel, and I'm about to dig a hole.
How long will they mourn me—until I get old.
You took people out of my life, and you left me in the fog.
I ain't tripping about dat—you still my dawg.

I'm standing in the rain with a blood clot in my brain,
yellin' out to you, Lord, please take away the pain.
You put something heavy on my back, and it felt like a log,
but you still my dawg,

Yeah, you still my dawg.

You came to my dream, and you told me this,
"Torrence, you still my dawg even after your life is dismissed."

Why Did God Take Her Away From Me?

Christine, 17
Christian (Catholic)

My mother was sick, and nobody knew what it was. In the back of my mind, I thought, "She's going to be fine. Everything is great."

And when my mom died, my whole family was there in the hospital. A priest was there, and we prayed over her as she literally took her last breath. I was just so out of it. I sat there holding hands with the people next to me, and I just cried, and I wasn't even thinking about the prayer. I wasn't thinking about anything.

There was a funeral mass. There was a wake. And at that point, I really was not into my faith at all. I was sort of numb. I sat through it, and I cried a lot. But the word "God" didn't mean anything to me at all.

When my mom died, I was fourteen. I'm the oldest. My brother and sister—we're all really close in age. Now we're fifteen, sixteen, and seventeen. My mother and my father split up when I was about five. My dad wasn't around. She remarried when I was eleven. So we live with my stepfather.

The three of us used to fight all the time. All of a sudden, I became the one who was trying to break up the fights and keep things in order, as opposed to being kept in order by my mom. The thing that was running through my head was, "This wouldn't be happening if she was here. So why did God take her away from me?" I questioned, "OK, is there a God? And if there is, why is he doing this to me?"

There was a long period in that year when I was just so angry and so upset and I didn't know how to deal with it. I went through stages of drinking and stuff. I experimented to see if that would make me feel better.

I've been in Catholic schools since the first grade. My mom always thought that was important. We didn't have a lot of money, but she worked two jobs just so that we could be in Catholic schools when we lived down the street from a public school.

When I was younger, being Catholic just meant going through the motions—going to church with my mom, doing my theology homework, and stuff like that.

I folded my hands and said the "Our Father" when I had to at mass.[27]

But as I got older, as I was starting high school, I started to think about it and what it meant. I got more involved. I'd go to one teen mass and not do anything else for a little while. But there was a thinking process going through my head about faith and about religion. I was realizing the importance of it, realizing that God is not just this being that people pray to and this being that made the world. God was a being that I can have a personal relationship with.

When I started going to church, I saw all these people who were so happy even though they had similar struggles to mine. I had to figure out what they were doing, and it was their faith in God. So I ended up leaning on that instead.

I started getting involved in the youth group at my church. It ended up becoming my family. We have teen masses and all sorts of events. We go on camping trips and ski trips, and other fun stuff. I had these new friends that I could share my faith with. At school I have all sorts of friends. But we never really talked about God because it wasn't the cool thing to do.

I get up and go to church by myself on Sunday. I am a completely different person than I was—much better in the way I handle myself. I pray daily. It gives me a great sense of connection with God. This past summer, I went on a retreat as a leader, and I gave a talk on God's love and forgiveness. And in that talk, I explained about realizing God's love through my experiences with other people and through prayer.

There are a lot of people who think, "Oh, those teens, they don't know anything." But that's when you really start to understand what your faith is, and what it means to you. People at my age start questioning things. That is the most important time to start developing their faith. I want to be a youth minister—that's one of my goals. I'd encourage people to explore what their faith means to them, rather than just going through the motions, as I used to do, and just going to church because their parents tell them to.

Faith is not just church. It's not just this institution that gives people something to belong to. That's part of it, but I think people often disregard the most important thing, which is the feeling that your faith in God can give you.

After my mom died, my faith sort of slapped me in the face and really became a part of my life. **When I look back, I see that God taking away my**

---

[27] The "Our Father," also known as the Lord's Prayer, is one of the most common prayers in Catholicism.

mother was actually almost good for me because of what I've gained from it.

Of course, it hurts. It's one of the worst things that could happen to somebody. But, at the same time, I've gained so much from the experience because of how I grew closer to God. God was all I had to fall back on, and prayer was all I had that was going to make me feel any better. It sort of became my safety blanket. And it became the central part of my life, whereas I think in the beginning it was just a wall to lean back on.

Take This Hopelessness Away from Me

Julie,* 20
Christian (nondenominational)
* not her real name

There have been times when I've been depressed. And a lot of times I've been suicidal. When I was nineteen, I had had an argument with my dad. I don't remember what the argument was about, but it left me feeling really down. I felt like the people I loved most in the world were against me. Depression keeps you awake sometimes. I remember lying on my bed until three o'clock in the morning that night. I remember being so, so depressed and feeling so, so hopeless. I think that was the deepest, darkest time in my life.

But there must have been some part of me that wanted to live because I remember praying—not even a cognitive prayer, I didn't even realize I was praying. Jesus kept giving me hope. I thought, "It doesn't matter if there is nobody else in the world who loves me, because Jesus is the lover of my soul. Nobody else is going to love me perfectly, and only Jesus can." That really helped. Even at my deepest, darkest moments, I've felt God lifting me up—I've actually felt it. I remember just crying out to God to take this hopelessness away from me. And he has.

God is like a father to me. Do you remember when you were a child and your daddy would smile at you and you'd feel his love? It's like that feeling. You're aware of his presence, and that's what I mean by drawing closer to him. It's like a more-perfect father than any of us knows just sitting there smiling at you. And when you're down, he puts an arm around your shoulder and helps you up and helps you through it. He's always there for you; it's just like a dad's love. That's the best I can do to describe his presence.

I went through some really tough times last year. And I still struggle some-times because you can't see him—you just have to trust. But over the last two years, it's been like I can feel his presence. I started going to midweek Bible study again about a month ago, and it's like he's there again and I can feel him. I guess when you draw close to God, he draws closer to you. He's always there protecting you. But you can't really get the full benefit of it unless you're drawn close to him.

Sometimes you're so overwhelmed by it you just want to sing and praise him. It's just overwhelming that a God that great and that omniscient and omnipresent would actually deign to look at me, because I'm just a small per-son among millions and millions of people. I don't deserve to be a Christian. There's nothing I've done, it's everything God's done for me. I didn't deserve to have Christ die on the cross. Since it's nothing I've done, I just want to go out and share it with other people. That's my spiritual story.

Cling, Cling to God!

Martin, 17
Christian

I was one of those kids—I used to tease people when I saw people wor-shipping God. When I saw people crying, or if they caught the Holy Ghost, I would tease people.

At the time I was like blowing up. I was getting bigger because a lot of fam-ily members had died. It seemed like family members were just dropping like flies. I lost two aunts, an uncle. I lost a cousin. I lost another uncle. I didn't know how to cope. All these aunts and uncles—they were like second parents to me. It really hurt me, and I was looking for a way out. So I was taking food as a way out. It was like escaping and not having to think about stuff.

One day I was sitting in the pew, just stuffing my face with candy. And at the end of the service this pastor said, "Cling to God like you cling to that thing that you feel is your friend and won't ever let you down. You feel that your God has failed you—God will never fail you. Cling, cling to God!"

It was like the room—the room was electric. It was like someone had set it on fire. **I felt a surge in me, and I just immediately began to cry, and I couldn't stop crying. I was just overwhelmed. It was like something hit me.**

It was like my body just walked up there. My mind was in another place, and I just walked. I got baptized.

That was an experience I'll never forget. That's how I got saved. If it wasn't for that, I probably wouldn't be sitting here right now.

Death Is Simply a Part of the Circle of Life

Darcy, 23
Jewish (Modern Orthodox)

My mother worked part time when I was little, so my father took care of me. He was a master craftsman and jeweler and an incredible parent and teacher. I'm definitely my father's daughter. I go into Home Depot, and I instantly gravitate to the power tools. I love fixing things and exploring, like him. He had such style, his pieces were unique. I prefer his jewelry.

Last August my father went into a coma and was taken to the hospital. I flew back to Colorado right away. After a week in the coma, his heart just stopped, and they couldn't keep it going, and he died.

It's funny, because when he died, the rabbi and our friends were very concerned that I would be angry at G-d for his death. But I never was. I was occasionally angry with my father for his timing—I wish he could be there when I get married, or have his first grandchild, every little milestone. I was never angry with G-d for taking him, or my father for going.

There's a phrase that Jews say when they receive any really bad news or when somebody dies, which is "Blessed are you, G-d, King of the Universe, the judge of truth." For me, that's very profound, because you're not saying it's not a terrible thing, a huge tragedy. You are acknowledging that, yes, it is a terrible thing, but ultimately, it's right, and G-d judges truthfully. Death is simply a part of the circle of life—you're born, you live, you die. And it was his time to die. It's sad for us who are still here because we miss him, but it's not a tragedy.

Oddly enough, my father's death actually strengthened my faith.

Death and Mourning

In Judaism there are a lot of rituals associated with death and mourning and burial. There's a very detailed list of what everybody does and how everything is done. **It's actually very comforting to have all the rules and all the decisions laid out and made for you, listed by law. It's a time when you're a wreck, you are incapable of making complex decisions, and you don't have to.** It's much easier to just mourn and not be distracted.

When the person dies, you bury them as soon as possible—within twenty-four hours, unless it's on the Sabbath, in which case you have to wait until Sabbath is over. My father died 4 A.M. on Friday morning, so we had a huge scramble so we could get everything ready so we could bury before Sabbath, 4 P.M.

We didn't have to pick out a coffin because all Jews use the same kind of coffin—it's just a plain pine box, no ornamentation, no lining. The body is meant to decay, so we don't preserve it with embalming fluid or satin-lined coffins that won't be eaten away. Everything is meant to fall apart.

Until it's buried, the body is attended at all times by someone Jewish, called a *shomer*, or guard, who sits either in the same room or in an adjoining room with the door ajar. This is done out of respect for the dead. People are inherently worthy of respect—this doesn't change just because they die. In death, too, they certainly deserve dignity. They aren't a slab of meat.

Unlike Christian burials, we fill in the grave ourselves, instead of leaving it for the cemetery workers. The casket is lowered in, and the family throws the first shovels of dirt onto it. After the family doesn't want to shovel anymore, members of the community take turns filling it in. Only when the grave is totally filled in do people leave. If you just leave the casket sitting there and you walk away and the workers come later and fill it in, you can still entertain some hope that they're not really dead, that it's just a big joke. But if you actually bury the casket yourself, you can't possibly entertain that hope anymore.

It was not as hard as we thought it would be to shovel the dirt. My mother and I thought we would both burst into tears instantly at the hollow thud of the dirt hitting the box, but we didn't.

Sitting Shivah

After that, the family goes back home, and we sit shivah, which is a week of mourning when our house is open for most of the day, and everybody stops by and visits and usually brings food. The family sits close to the ground on low chairs or stools. I sat on the floor a lot. Some say you sit close to the ground because there is still an attachment to the deceased, and you feel closer this way.

While you sit shivah, you don't do anything or go anywhere. You aren't supposed to leave your house unless it's really urgent. You don't shower unless you're physically dirty, because bathing makes you feel good. You cover up all the mirrors in the house so you aren't distracted with unimportant things like how you look. You don't change clothes unless they are dirty or smell bad. You really don't get dirty or smelly because you aren't moving around since you can't go anywhere. The whole point is to mourn. This is time set aside to officially acknowledge that your life has changed in a very fundamental way, and to give you time to mourn and think about the deceased and talk about them, without being distracted by your normal daily affairs.

For the first eleven months after the death, the sons of the deceased are supposed to go to synagogue every day, twice a day if they can, and say the Kaddish prayer with a quorum of ten men. You can't say it without the quorum. If there are no sons, or none who will assume the obligation, a daughter may voluntarily assume it, but is not obligated. I assumed it as a way of honoring my father; to me this was the last thing I could do for my father in this life. I don't always make it twice a day, but the required minimum of once a day at least. It takes about one hour for the morning service and another hour for the afternoon/evening service. I have to get up every morning at seven to go to synagogue for services.

The Kaddish is a prayer that mourners say that actually says nothing about the dead. It's basically just a sanctification of G-d's name. It's normally a part of the service at set places. There are a couple versions of it, and some of them anyone can say, and others only mourners should say. When we get to the place where mourners say it, one person will lead the others and all the mourners will recite it together at the same time.

There's different arguments about whether saying Kaddish benefits the survivors because it helps them come to terms with the death or if it helps the soul of the departed. Some people say it doesn't do anything for the soul of the departed—they're dead. It's just for your own benefit. Either way, I found it very nice, very comforting. Usually there are several mourners saying it with you, so it becomes its own community of mourners. It's also nice to have time that's set aside out of every day specifically for you to think about the departed.

During the year of mourning, the children of the deceased have the strictest obligations and are not allowed to do anything in public that is "fun." It's custom more than law, but I'm not supposed to go out and have fun or do anything during the entire year—no parties, no dancing, no theater. I don't go out and watch movies anymore. If I want to watch movies, I can rent a DVD and watch it at home. When I moved into my apartment, I couldn't even have a housewarming party.

I was in synagogue this morning and realized that on June 24 I will not go to synagogue, since that is when the eleven months of saying Kaddish end, and I almost started crying in the middle of services again. It's not hard to stop going, since it is very difficult now to take large chunks out of my day, every day, to schedule *minyan*.[28] But I do it because it's for my father and this is the last honor I can show him in this life, aside from occasionally giving charity. I've found it's actually very helpful.

It will be hard to stop going because it's symbolic of the fact that the year is coming to an end. And in a way, it feels to me like I'm putting my father aside—he ceases to be an active daily part of my life—in an official, scheduled way. Now I just have memories. And that's going to be really hard because I'm not quite ready to put my father aside.

But every year, you remember this person. For the rest of my life, I'll go to synagogue on the anniversary, which will be sometime around the end of July, beginning of August on the Gregorian calendar (this year excepting), say Kaddish prayer, and light a Yahrzeit candle at home, which burns for twenty-four hours. It's not like, "He died five years ago, who remembers anymore?" It's like, "He died five years ago, and tomorrow is the day, and I have to light a candle."

A growing body of research supports the idea that religious practices—prayer, Shabbat observance for Jews, and participation in the rituals of the Eucharist for Catholics, for example—are vitally important, says James Fowler. "We've often heard it said that you act your way into new ways of believing more readily than you think your way into them. That's what practices are about—they're acting your way into faithfulness. . . . Practices help the images and the language of faith to become internalized and to become part of the rhythm of your lives."

Religious practices create "a rhythm of life that intersperses contemplation and restoring the soul in the midst of busy and outgoing lives."

---

[28] Minyan is Hebrew for prayer quorum.

It's This Overwhelmingly Serene Moment

Adina, 16
Jewish (Conservative)

Lighting the candles for Shabbat is one of my favorite things to do. You do this on Friday night, right before Sabbath dinner, as the sun is going down.[29] It's a really girl thing to do.

I light two candles, and my mom lights two, and my little sister would light two. But some of my friends do one for every person in the household, or one for every kid, because they bring light into your life. Each person lights one, or one person lights all. And you wave your hands around the candles three times after they are lit to draw the light into your soul.

You can't strike a match on Shabbat. So you have to light the candles and then cover your eyes and say the blessing to bless the coming of the Sabbath.[30] The English translation of the blessing is: "Blessed are you, Lord our God, King of the Universe, who has sanctified us with his commandments and commanded us to light the Shabbat candles." I say it in Hebrew with a melody, but I can't carry a tune very well.

And then you can look at the flame. You take this moment to reflect. A lot of women take that moment to pray to God about their household. I reflect on the week that has occurred and what I hope will come the next week. Sometimes I just try to clear my mind and allow the peacefulness of Shabbat to flow into my soul.

My dad lives by himself, and he lights the candles every week. But he likes to have me there to help him when I'm there on his weekends.

However you want to do it, it's this overwhelmingly serene moment where you get to block things out. It's really calming. That's when you know the week's over.

---

[29] The exact time that the candles are lit varies from household to household. Some families light the candles just before the Sabbath meal. The traditional time is eighteen minutes before sunset.

[30] Under Jewish law, a blessing is given before an action; that is, the blessing would be said before the action—the lighting of the Shabbat candles. But once the blessing is said, Shabbat begins, and Jewish law forbids lighting a fire on the Sabbath. To get around this, the candles are lit, and then the eyes are covered when the blessing is given.

My Battery Is Recharged

Dan, 20
Jewish

Sometimes you just need to disconnect, to sit back and have a good time, eat good food, rest, and be with friends. Shabbat allows me to forget about everything that I've been surrounding myself with for the week—my paper that's due Tuesday, or my test that's due Monday, this application that's due whenever, or other things that may cause stress at any given time.

It allows me to disconnect myself from the outside world for just twenty-four hours and connect myself with God, connect myself with the religion, connect myself with the community. And then come Saturday night, I'm refreshed and my battery is recharged and I can go for the rest of the week.

I have friends who have been observing Shabbat since they were young; they grew up in observant households. What is Saturday for them? It's the restrictions. It's "I can't watch Saturday-morning cartoons." And it has bothered me sometimes. Sometimes I say to myself, "Oh, man! If I had Saturday to work on my paper, what a breather that would be." But I plan for things. If I know that I have a paper due on Monday, and I'm not going to be working between Friday night and Saturday night, then I start on Friday afternoon or Thursday afternoon.

As I've grown older, and as I've been surrounded with deadlines and pressure—this and that tugging on me from all directions—Shabbat has been one of the greatest things that I have ever had. And I would go nuts if I didn't have that break.

It's My Sanctuary

Daniel, 21
Christian (Catholic)

I work all day Saturday. And so I get up at 11:30 on Sunday, shower, and I go to mass. Sometimes I listen and I try to pay attention. Other times, I just kind of sit there and relax. It's the one place in my entire life where I don't have somebody asking me to do something or yelling at me about something. I just go there and kind of collect my thoughts.

Because when you're at work or when you're at home, it's like: It's 6:30. We have to be at this barbecue. And at 7:00, I gotta call Tim. And after that, we have to go to this bar and pick up this guy. And what do I gotta do next week? What books do I have to read?

At church it's so slow that I can just relax for a second, and gather my thoughts, and gain some clarity. I hope it's from the fact that it's a holy place and it's easier to be calm there and gain insight and things. It could just be that it's my sanctuary. And it feels like I gain something from being in the presence of other people who believe.

Christ Has Risen!

Antonios, 24
Christian (Greek Orthodox)

I think Easter is my favorite holiday. It's a very important holiday. I love going to church during Easter. Every other day of the year, you go to church on Sunday and it's full, but nowhere near as full as Easter. Even at Christmas, church doesn't fill up. It's good to see that everybody is coming to pray.

Every year I go to Easter service at St. Demetrios in Chicago. That's where our whole family grew up—that was our church, that's where everybody got married, that's where all us kids got baptized. It's a very pretty church. The icons, the architecture of the church, the chandeliers—it's gorgeous to look at. Everything is gold and very colorful.

It's full of stories. There are pictures painted on the walls, pictures of all the different saints and the different events that took place. As you look at the walls, certain events come back—some of the stories you learned about.

The service is Greek upstairs and English downstairs. But most of the time the service is in both. Most of the younger generation does not understand everything in Greek. And now we're getting more diverse races of people in the Greek Orthodox churches in Chicago. You see a variety of people. We have African-Americans. We have Oriental people. We have all kind of people coming to our church now.

I go to church every night for seven days before Easter. They have a different liturgy every night. On Friday night, you sing the hymn for when they put the Lord on the cross. It's sad, it's touching. That's when they put him in the tomb when he dies. They bring out the tomb, and we walk around outside the church. Our tomb is like a little square hut. It has a picture icon of the crucified Lord and it's decorated with flowers. At the end of the service everybody takes a flower.

On Saturday night, you're still in mourning. The priest is still talking about the resurrection and praying for the resurrection. Then midnight comes, that's when the Lord has left the tomb and he is now among us again. He has come back to life. That's when the priest takes the flame from the candle that sits back there where we have the icons of the Lord. He hands it to the altar boys, and they pass around the eternal flame of life throughout the gathered people in the church. Everybody lights their candles. And that's the flame that everybody brings home with them that night. Then you sing, "Christ has risen!" And we rejoice. You just feel good. You pray for the Lord to be with you for the whole year.

On Easter you eat a lot, you can eat anything you want. You fast up until Easter. We have forty days of fasting during Lent. We stay away from eating meat, oils, and all dairy products for forty days. A lot of us lose weight during that time. We eat olives, and they have certain foods you can get at Greek stores. My mom makes bread with flour and water. We have plain rice, noodles. You can't avoid everything, but you try your best. For the young people who are not married, there's celibacy for forty days.

I'm more in touch with God during that holiday. I go to church. I go to confession. I pray every day. I thank the Lord for everything he's given me. I pray for forgiveness. I ask him to keep everybody in my family healthy and watch over us. It makes me feel good, being at church that much. I think that religion makes me feel better. It makes your soul feel good.

Everyone Is Praying, Fasting, and Doing Good

Tuba, 18
Muslim

Religion in My Life

It is impossible for me to pinpoint just one aspect of my religion that I enjoy doing most. For me, religion is my life. It really is a way of life. A lot of my goals, my ambitions, are formed by Islam.

For me, and for most Muslims who are serious about their religion, our ultimate goal in life is to serve God so well that we attain paradise and are saved from hell. For Muslims, this life is a test. After we die, we are given the results of how we did in this life—whether we did good, or whether we did bad. There's going to be the Day of Judgment, where everyone will be given their final judgment—whether you will go to heaven, whether you will go to hell. You might reside in both for a certain period of time, or only in one—for eternity.

Paradise is a place that we achieve in the next life. In our holy book, paradise is described as a garden with drinks and fruits, that even though we know of them from Earth, the taste of them are more exquisite than anything we've tasted. It's really a place of pure happiness where you reside in forever.

So for me, every action I do will either help me to gain paradise or will keep me away from it. And when you have that in mind, especially when you're praying five times a day, it does help form who you are.

One of my favorite times is the approaching of the month of Ramadan. It causes a lot of excitement within the community. Ramadan is our holy month. It's the month when the Qur'an, our holy book, was first revealed. So this month is quite a blessing for us.

Every Muslim who is mature and sane and able must fast from dawn till sunset. You abstain from eating and drinking. That's the more physical part of it. It's more than just not eating and drinking. It's really abstaining from doing other things which are wrong or forbidden or immoral. And Muslims believe that because we're all doing this together, it prevents us from getting deceived very easily by Satan.

Everyone's praying and fasting and doing good and reminding each other to do good. Ramadan is the month when Muslims give the most to charity.

Also during this month, there is a tradition where we pray additional prayers during the night. Some people pray on their own. But there's also the prayers at the mosque. I enjoy praying with others because I get to share with them some part of their spirituality. It helps to strengthen my own.

For a lot of Muslims, when Ramadan is over you feel really sad. It's a whole month when all your blessings were doubled, when you were engaging so much in prayer, and the community would come every night for extra prayers. It's pretty sad, especially if you felt you didn't exert yourself as much as you could have and didn't get as many rewards as you could have.

When Eid comes along, it kind of diminishes that sadness and establishes a more cheerful optimistic feeling.[31] Eid is the day after Ramadan. You have a congregational prayer with everyone in the community. It's really cool because you see so many people.

Prayer

For me, praying at night, during Ramadan and outside of Ramadan, is very spiritually uplifting. What I'm talking about is praying deep into the night, or right before we pray the dawn prayer, before anyone else is up. No one sees me, no one hears me. I can cry if I want to, do what I want to, without having any eyes on me. I just feel more close to God. I can put things in perspective—life's not ending because of a little problem here or there.

Almost every time I pray, it's for gratefulness for everything I have. And there's also paradise, which we strive for. I know it's impossible to reach without divine intervention, without divine guidance. So I pray for that. I pray for forgiveness and for my family members. Day before yesterday, I was up for a lot of the night. Around 3 A.M., I was laying in bed still, so I just began praying for everyone in my family. And by praying for them and asking for their blessings, I realized my own blessings in having them, and their worth, their goodness.

I pray for whatever is on my mind. It ranges from a higher ACT score, to making me better friends with someone I'm not getting along with too well, to praying for my nieces, to praying for the people in the U.S. and the world who are oppressed, and praying for my own ambitions and my dreams of how I want to improve the world.

---

[31] Eid, also referred to as *Id al-Fitr*, is a celebration following Ramadan. Muslims decorate their homes, exchange gifts, visit friends and family, and prepare holiday meals.

Power and intellectual challenge are some of the other benefits that people derived from the beliefs and practices of their faith.

It's a Big Driving Force

Oz, 20
Muslim

There was a time in my life when I was a rebellious teenager, and during that time I said, "Forget about religion, I'm just going to go out and figure it out for myself." I did believe that there was something else, somewhere else, but I had to go find it. And I came here [the United States]. I've set my mind to do something here—start work and make a lot of money and be successful.

What made me choose to have faith again was the realization that having religion, faith, makes you more powerful. It gives you power to deal with things. When you believe that some greater force is behind things, when you believe there is more than just muscle power or brainpower to you, when you think there is something that guides you, something you get inspired from without even realizing it—when you think that something like that exists—it's a big driving force. People achieve great things through having faith in some higher power. It helps you get through depression, tough times in your life. It helps you create. It's a very innovative force. And when I saw this, I was like, "Hey, do I want this power or not?"

It's a trade-off. The price that you pay for accepting this power is convincing yourself that certain things exist, and therefore leading an unscientific life, which was hard for me. I'm a science person, and there is this inherent objectivism, realism, that you have to have to be a science person. That conflicts with the whole idea of religion, which is to believe in something you cannot feel or touch or measure. From a scientific perspective, faith is not reliable because it's not solid. That's the conflict.

I'm a Muslim, and I love Islam. My interpretation of Islam, my own religion, is very success oriented. If I have faith in myself, in the God inside me, I will be successful. And this is a driving force. Religion is very motivating in that sense. I think religion is basically a way to convince yourself to go out there and do things.

The Power of Faith

Every time before a final, there is a point when studying is done and you can't really be constructive anymore by trying to push more into your brain. And at that point, my faith helps me because I like to think that there is actually this big thing that I'm a part of, that I'm connected to. And whatever knowledge I will need on the test, it's somewhere out there. And since I'm connected to everything including that, I'll be able to figure it out. And this belief helps me.

In the test, if there's something I really don't know, I think and try to tap into this thing that's a part of me and that's also part of the universe. It's like the process of thinking and trying to find the answer is like trying to reach God, and through that I get a lot of answers. People often say in religious writings, "God told me something." I think they were just thinking by themselves and realized something.

Talking with God

I have an ongoing conversation with God. I think everybody has. People call it different things. It's an internal dialogue. It's a dialogue with something, maybe just myself even. But I justify things through that dialogue and unjustify certain things. So that dialogue gives me an idea of right and wrong, which makes me think it's very related to religion. That's the only form of prayer that I pursue, and I do that all the time.

When you're choosing a religion or you're making one up, you should think of what your goals are. Islam was the best for me because it fits my goals. It can be interpreted to drive you to wherever you want to go. Islam is so open to interpretation.

The Qur'an is a very good source of knowledge, just like the Bible is. You can see a lot of humanity in it, read it and see amazing human responses. It was sent to us or written—whatever you want to believe, it doesn't even matter where it comes from. It's a guidebook to life. But you don't need to apply it exactly as it is written.

To be honest, there were parts of it that didn't really apply to me. I think it should be a part of religion to filter the content that you're getting from it. Don't take anything at face value; question everything—maybe that's the lesson to take from religion. Take parts you understand and want to apply and just filter out the rest if it doesn't apply, or doesn't make sense, or if others are not understanding it.

In the later stage of my life, when I no longer want to have this drive for success, and maybe I will just want happiness and peace, I think I can just change the interpretation a little bit and make it a little more peaceful set of beliefs.

The Traditional Texts Are Really Important to Me

Lauren,* 22
Jewish (Orthodox)
*not her real name

Learning is a big thing. When we say, "What are you doing this summer?" you say, "Learning." It refers to a specific kind of activity—sitting all day looking at a page of Talmud or commentaries, trying to figure out what they say. And it's one of the most important things that you can do.

I don't necessarily buy the idea that in the most literal sense, learning Torah changes the world or that by learning Torah you're learning the specific word of God. I don't think that everything that's written in the Talmud was sent to Moses. I do think that there's an interpretive tradition—not the content, but the way that you study—that has to be passed on.

The traditional texts are really important to me, and the vocabulary of the texts and the way people read them has a lot to do with the way I think and the way I approach problems. I see this as a fascinating way of conveying ideas. It grabs me.

There's this passage in the midrash—midrash being commentaries on the Bible and older material written from the third century to the twelfth century—where they talk about the creation of man. Justice and Peace met and faced each other, and Abundance/Loving Kindness and Truth faced each other. In other similar midrashim, it's not these attributes, but angels whom God asks for advice about creating man.

When God wanted to create man, the angels were divided evenly over the question. Justice and Loving Kindness said, "Yes, that's a great idea." Justice said, "He can mete out justice," and Loving Kindness said, "He can do kindness for the world." Some said, "No, you should not create him." Truth said man is all lies, and Peace said man creates war.

They were even—two against two. God, who really just asked them as a formality, was like, "Fine, you don't want man to be created." And he took

Truth and threw it out of heaven to Earth. And then he was like, "It's two against one. We can create man." We have this proof text for the fact that God threw Truth out of heaven to Earth, because the Bible elsewhere says that Truth shall spring up from the ground. This is just a snippet. Obviously something like this has a lot of depth.

God Throws Out Truth

It's a really big question—what does it mean to say things like that about God? For me, the most interesting thing is: how does throwing Truth out solve the question? For me, part of the way it solves the question is by changing the nature of truth. You take truth from this thing that exists in heaven to this thing that lives on the Earth—this thing that is fluid, it moves, and grows up.

These texts are a good example of how a specific kind of narrative can carry a lot of ideas. When you want to say something about truth, especially in philosophy, you don't tell a story like that, and you certainly don't tell a story with so many gaps. In comparison, I think the intellectual world of the academy is very stale in many respects. The questions of theology are sort of cognitive questions like, "What does it mean to talk about God after X or before X?" It's a very almost dry question.

There's something you can get out of the way a story is told—not having things spelled out, having things phrased in terms of very ambiguous relationships. What I enjoy about reading these texts is how you can read them in an alive way. You have to be actively involved. I find it really fun, because I'm an intellectual person.

It's also important to understand the kind of logic that's behind the Jewish legal system that we have today, which is not the same kind of logic that's behind most of the rest of our lives. There are certain formalisms and ways of thinking. In some ways they're classical.

I just read this article by Emmanuel Levinas, who was a Jewish French philosopher. It was called "Loving the Torah More Than God." That title is revealing because within Orthodoxy, there are these texts that are very spiritual—even if they don't directly relate to God—and there's this whole group of practices.

I think those things can substitute for a religious life in the absence of a clear idea of what God is, in the sense that if you buy into the system, then you accept the idea that these things will point you on your way. So you can focus on these things for the time being, and try and figure out where that leaves you in abstract religious terms later.

Young people who grow up in certain circumstances benefit more from their involvement in a church, mosque, or synagogue than others, says Stephen Warner. For example, youth from low-income families tend to benefit more than youth from affluent families. That's because religious institutions are some of the few places in low-income communities that offer kids a safe place to play, tutoring, and other opportunities for growth and recreation.

"It may be, 'Hey, that's where the basketball court is' or 'Hey, that's where I can sit around in the afternoon and not get hit upon by some guy.' So religion is a safe place," says Warner. "The further down you are on the social ladder, the more religion is a material force for good. If you don't have a lot of economic privilege in your life, religion can be a huge factor in your either finishing high school or being dead."

Also, kids growing up in dysfunctional homes or with single parents who are away at work can benefit from religious involvement. In houses of worship, adults often take on roles as counselors, coaches, and in the case of men, even substitute dads. "It's one place kids can go to find adults they can trust," says Warner.

They Look Out for Me

Aaron,* 14
Christian
*not his real name

Me and my sisters—we always say we're gonna write a book about our life and go on *Oprah*, because we've been through a lot. My story seems kind of complex sometimes, but compared to my sisters, they've been through so much more. We've been to a lot of schools. I've been to like seven or eight. My older sister went to like thirteen. We moved around a lot.

A lot of people always say, "Were your parents in the service or something?" They just liked to move, they don't like to stay in one place. They just burned their bridges so many times that people don't want to help them anymore, so they'll go somewhere else where people don't know them.

When I was twelve, things just weren't going right. Father just got out of jail and was trying to preach. He told me that he was going to be a pastor. I understand it's possible to get saved in jail—they have services and everything—but I just didn't feel that it was right. But then he moved down to Florida, and he got a girlfriend. My mom said, "Everything's going to be all right." I thought, "No, this is not the place for me. I need to be some place stable. I can't live like this."

My mom asked me what I wanted to do. I said, "I love you, Mom. I love Dad. But I don't feel this is the place for me, because I can't be stable with you guys because you guys are forever moving." I had to figure out how to get out of there. I was trying to come up here [Chicago] and stay with my grandmother. I talked to a social worker, and she paid for a ticket for me to come back here. My mom was mad, but she let me go. So I came up here.

I didn't live with my parents for about three or four years. I visited them a few times. I stayed with my grandmother. I stayed with my godparents. Then my godparents thought I could stay with my biological parents, that they're able to take care of me. I had to move back with my parents, and I didn't really like that idea, but I didn't have any choice. I didn't like the idea, because I liked my situation in Chicago and where I was living.

It's Like a Family

I've been having some problems since I've been down here. I really love my church in Chicago. It's like a family. They help each other out when things are going wrong. A lot of times I need that because I have a lot of family problems. When you're there, you don't have to worry about your problems. A lot of times you don't think about your outside life. And that really helps a lot.

I had to come back to that because I stopped going to church when I first got down here. Everybody was trying to force me to go to church, and I didn't like that because I'm old enough to decide that on my own. After I got out of my stubbornness, I started going back. I've been going on my own.

I used to live here a couple years back, so I still know people. I'm really close to people. A lot of my friends here are older than me, eighteen to twenty-two. I met them in the church about seven years ago. They're kind of like brothers. I talk to them all the time, just to express myself. I talk to them about this situation. They listen. They give me ideas. I may be thinking of doing something, and they tell me, "Don't do that, because that could put you in a worse place than you are in." They look out for me.

A lot of times I will be having a problem with my mom and I don't want to talk to her. And I can go to church and I can hear a message—and it might even be for me. And after church, we all just come together and we socialize. And sometimes I need that. Like sometimes I need to come to church just for the aftereffects—for everyone to talk to and just say hi. When I have problems, it just takes it off my mind. I go to church, and then some of the guys, we go play basketball and just hang out together.

They Guided Me

Growing up in a south Chicago suburb known for high rates of poverty and crime, Pablo dropped out of school and joined a street gang. He credits the church, and the mentors he found there, for turning his life around.

Pablo, 24
Christian (Catholic)

We came from Mexico when I was young. I was about five. The problems of the neighborhood were that everybody was dropping out of school and a lot of them were joining gangs. Most of them were getting pregnant at very young ages. And of course, there was a lot of violence.

You get affected with these problems. I myself didn't finish high school. I was a sophomore when I left school. I was involved with the local gang for about a year or two. I joined in when I was thirteen and got out when I was about fifteen.

As a result of the violence around you, you had to join in on one side or the other. You couldn't stay neutral. If you stayed neutral, you pretty much got picked on anyways. You were going to get into a fistfight with somebody. You were going to commit some sort of violence against someone. You couldn't have any sense of morals, in the sense that it's wrong to hit somebody. You weren't thinking in the back of your head about the commandment "You shall not kill" or not hurting anybody. You were not thinking about any of that.

Drug use amongst the youth got really bad when I was a teen. It was mostly marijuana and cocaine. The thing that really got to me about the gang was the drug use. It was unbelievable how they put all that stuff in their bodies. I used drugs a couple of times, but they were using every day, on and on. They were selling—the selling was another thing I didn't like, and the fact that they were trying to recruit the younger kids in the neighborhood. I'm talking about twelve-year-olds, thirteen-year-olds. I didn't like that.

Saint Donatus is in Blue Island, which is one of the suburbs right next to Harvey. Some cousins of mine were going to the youth group there, and they invited me to come. As I kept going, I liked it. They didn't pray all the time. They presented issues, and they showed us how, through faith, we can overcome them—things like being depressed, or going through a breakup, or getting into a fight with your parents.

Gang vs. Youth Group

I was in the gang, and I was going to the youth group, and I was seeing the differences in lifestyle. In one lifestyle, you're always on the edge, always watching your back. In one lifestyle, you're more at peace—I really wanted that.

With faith, I always had like a little-kid mentality—the God that punishes, and the God that is always watching you if you're bad, and the heaven-and-hell deal. I wanted to learn more about how spirituality could help me. I met the youth leaders, and they began teaching me different ways of dealing with life problems through faith.

I learned that through prayer and through spiritual character, you can have a stable emotional life. You don't have to let the problems of your neighborhood bring you down. There is another way of life that is more peaceful, that's more in harmony with God, that has more hope. I was like: I want to leave the gang. I don't want to live like this.

Also, my family didn't know what I was doing. My mom believed that I was a good kid, and it bothered me because I wasn't. My mom was one of the main reasons why I decided to leave, and the fact that my dad had a lot of hopes for me. They left their country to give us something better, and here I was destroying it. Plus, I had my younger brothers—they looked up to me.

I knew the risks of leaving. I would need to go through a violation to get out, which is a beating. Another is I didn't have any place to go. If I just left the gang, they were going to come after me. They would think I might go tell the police on them.

The programs that supposedly help just weren't around. The only thing that was around was my cousin and the youth group at Saint Donatus. Marco was a seminarian there who was studying to be a priest. He would always come around and just talk to me. He didn't judge me. Besides a great friend, he was also a great spiritual mentor. Marco was like, "We need to take you out of the neighborhood because it's dangerous for you to stay there." They took me out of the neighborhood.

Getting Out

One of Marco's friends worked in a Comboni missionary seminary in Azusa, California. I stayed there for three months, and then I came back and I

MY FAITH JOURNEY

lived with one of my uncles in Blue Island for another two years. Being out of the neighborhood helped me reflect on my life and begin to change.

My faith gave me new strength. It gave me the strength to believe that I didn't have to stay where I was. I got my GED. I went to Moraine Valley Community College. I found some great people there. I started at a very low general education level, and I worked my way up, and I managed to get the associate's degree in liberal arts.

Most of the gang members I knew ended up in prison for a while. One of them passed away, he got shot. One or two became addicted to drugs. Most of them decided to leave the gang. A few stuck around and took leadership positions in the gang. In Harvey, and in other neighborhoods—Pilsen and Chicago Heights—the gangs are there. The unfortunate part is that they're recruiting. They're doing their business.

A Different Example

That is why I'm doing what I'm doing. I got involved in *Pastoral Juvenil*, Pastoral Youth Ministry, which is a network of the different movements of the archdiocese, dealing with Hispanic youth mostly.

What I'm doing right now in Harvey is working with a teenage group there. It's a way of meeting needs that otherwise would not be met in the neighborhood—like literally taking these kids, before they're recruited into a gang, and showing them something else. We show them that the neighborhood is bad but it doesn't have to be that way. And we show them the importance of continuing school, of not dropping out.

You get all kinds of youth. Harvey is predominantly African-American, and there's a small community of Polish-Americans, and recently there's been a lot of Mexican-Americans moving there. You get immigrant youth—literally sixteen-year-old kids that have decided to cross the border—and they can find friends here, and they can become part of a family in a way. You also have the kids that are just like me—I kind of see myself in their shoes. You also get girls that are just trying to find out what their role is as women in this world.

I try to give them a different example. I like the story of the rich man who was asked to give his belongings to follow Christ. I'm always reflecting on that story because it tells you that you have to give up everything—give it up, just follow him. I don't have millions of dollars, but there are things that hold me back from doing what I need to do—things like pride and selfishness.

I work hard when it comes to working with youth. When you get somebody who is going to give you a lot of trouble, you have to think to yourself, "I have to be very patient." Sometimes I'm like, "I'm not going to do this, because I don't like him," and I always go back to that story. My faith motivates me a lot to be a better person.

My Calling

My plan for the future is to get my master's in psychology. I believe my calling in this life is to help others. This is where I particularly find that the church is helpful for me, because it gives me the opportunity to give back to young kids. It has given me the chance to help friends of mine that were struggling with alcohol problems. It has given me the opportunity to help others, and that's something that I thank God for.

I've had some great mentors to help me that were involved with the youth ministry. When I had crises and difficulties—questions about the right path, the wrong path, or even how to identify either—they guided me. I believe that there is hope and that you can empower yourself and you can empower others through faith, through God.

Voices of Women

Dozens of girls and young women of different faiths that I spoke with grappled with similar issues. Some of them talked about patriarchal religious institutions that limited their role in worship. Some railed against the sexist views held by the males of their faith. And others—mostly Muslims—challenged the stereotypes about females of their faith held by many Americans.

Americans are familiar with images of veiled and covered Muslim women in Afghanistan, Saudi Arabia, and other faraway lands, along with stories about the oppressive treatment of women in these countries. As a result, many Americans equate Islam with the oppression of women. This notion infuriates and frustrates many of the Muslim women I spoke to.

Do I Act Oppressed?

Assia, 17
Muslim

I think Americans have the misconception that we're oppressed and that we're forced to do what we do.

The funniest thing happened to me once. Three years ago I was at my friend's older sister's house. I was outside with her kids, and I was watching them play. And this guy comes out on his balcony, and he's like, "You're in America! You're free. You can take your scarf off."

I was like, "What?"

Like they think that you have to wear the scarf. We have careers. We go to school. We drive cars. How can you think that we're oppressed? Do I look oppressed? Do I act oppressed? I think that's a huge misconception.

Islam liberated women. Women got the right to own their own property and divorce way before women in European countries did. We never needed feminism.

We do a lot of interfaith in Catholic schools. After they meet us, they're like, "Oh, when we first met you, we thought you were forced to wear the scarves and you were forced to be the way you are." And then they see that we choose to do what we do.

Don't Pity Us

Maham, 19
Muslim [Ahmadi]

I know that there's a lot of pity for Muslims. People pity Muslim women because they have to wear the hijab. And to them I would say, "Don't pity us, because today, women who wear the headscarves choose to wear the headscarves. It's a choice. Everything is a choice."

You can go to any other country, like Saudi Arabia or Egypt or Turkey—women there choose to wear the headscarf. I'd say to Americans, "Admire them because they are doing something I bet none of us have the guts to do." I'd like to see people here be forced to get to know girls by their actions and not by the way they look.

I always say that women in Islam who wear headscarves are more liberated than women in America who choose to paint themselves up every day. I'm guilty of that, too. We worry about what we're going to wear, how we look, how our hair is—that's not being liberated, that's being restrained by expectations that have been set up for us.

In Islam, all the women are dressed modestly. The headscarf is all about modesty. We are forced to deal with women's actions and who they are and their minds, instead of what they look like. **Deal with my mind, not my body. I don't think it brings women down.**

A woman is supposed to unveil herself in front of her husband—that's the only man she should be attracting. In their houses, where their husbands are, [non-Muslim] women will wear sweatpants and look like scum. When they are going out to a party, where there are other men, they put on lipstick and a nice dress. It should be the other way around.

Christianity teaches modesty. Christian women are also supposed to cover themselves—the way nuns have for centuries. It's just not enforced anymore. Even Jewish women who are Orthodox wear long skirts and present themselves modestly. It's all about modesty, and I just wish people would see that sometimes.

When I spoke to Muslims about being Muslim and being female, they rarely expressed any misgivings about the role of women in their faith—until I spoke with a group of teens at a local mosque.

The girls were in transition between being girls and being women. They were noticing new attention from the opposite sex, as well as new restrictions and responsibilities that were not shared by the boys their age.

They Shouldn't Be . . . Looking Down Our Shirts.

Jasmina, 16
Meliha, 14
Amina, 12
Muslim

Amina: If you're a girl, you can't date someone who's Christian. But if you're a boy, you can date a girl who's Christian.

Meliha: The girl can change her religion for a guy. The male has more power.

Jasmina: Women are expected to stay home and clean, like help their moms out, and dress properly. If a woman is not dressed properly, then if a man looks at you, it's your fault because you're kind of leading him on.

Even though you don't think anybody is going to look at you, people do look at you. So it's up to a girl to watch how she dresses and to not show a lot of her body. And she's not supposed to date other religions.

I can date, but my mom is really strict about it. In Arabic countries, you cannot date at all. It's really strict. They have arranged marriages and everything. But in Bosnia, it's different. They are also Muslims, but you don't see a lot of people wearing scarves, like in the Arabic countries. Once you get really old, you start wearing scarves and praying every single day.

Meliha: Or if they go on hajj. When you come back from hajj, it's kind of like a routine—you have to start wearing a scarf and start praying. You can't come back from hajj and then go around being who you were before that.

Amina: You have to be really careful what you do around boys, even if it's in your house, with your dad, your brothers. You have to be careful how you sit . . . it's like you have to do all these proper things.

When I was in Bosnia last year, I was wearing shorts 'cause it's hot in the summer. My mom yelled at me. She told me, "Go change," because there were guys there. She was like, "You're starting to grow up, so you can't be around them."

Meliha: Like my mom, she keeps on saying, "You're growing up. You have to start changing yourself." But what am I supposed to wear? Sweatpants and a long-sleeved shirt during the summer when it's like 90 degrees outside?

We can't always help it. Shorts—I don't find that a problem. You're just exposing your legs . . . that's how you're comfortable.

We have to change ourselves for other people. We shouldn't have to change. We have our life. The guys shouldn't be looking at us, like looking down our shirts, or whatever. My parents tell me I should start thinking about it more—how you should dress appropriately toward your religion. I'm probably going to change that soon. At one point, I will start wearing a scarf and I'll start dressing more appropriately. Once you get to this age, you start understanding what you expect of your religion and you start following it more.

Jasmina: Every action that a woman does, everything that happens—it's basically the woman's fault. They always blame it on you and say, "You shouldn't have done that." You're expected to do so much.

I see where this is coming from. And I kind of understand why my parents are trying to keep me away from stuff, like dating different kinds of people. I know that they've been through a lot and they know what kind of people are out there.

But sometimes I think it's not fair how I have to go inside so early. When it gets dark, my dad's like, "OK, it's dark." I'm like, "It's only eight o'clock. All my friends stay out late." And he's like, "Trust me. You can be mad at me. You can even hate me. But one day you're going to thank me, and you're going to be the same parent I am if you really care about your kids." Our religion requires a lot. There are a lot of rules for us. One day, we see that all of this is worth it. God is something bigger than all this.

Meliha: My friend, she's Christian. Her parents are divorced. Her mom is never around. And she's pregnant two months, and she's only fourteen. Now all of a sudden, she started doing drugs, and she's going around with other guys.

My parents are so strict, and I'm so happy for that. They keep me away from that.

On the following pages, a young woman expresses frustration at what she views as sexual discrimination in Conservative Judaism. Another woman argues that what is perceived as discrimination is actually something very different.

They Don't Want to Listen to Women's Voices

Serena,* 17
Jewish (Conservative)
* not her real name

You can call me a Conservative Jew, but I went to this discussion on Conservative Judaism, and when I came out of it, I was like, "I don't know why I'm a Conservative Jew." We say that we're this pluralistic movement and we accept everyone—except women, except homosexuals, and except . . .

I belong to a youth group. One of our leaders is very right, compared to the movement, and he is very against women. He won't let women do things. He and I have issues because he doesn't like that I infringe on his authority because I know things and I'm a girl.

I have a background; I went to a Jewish day school. I had the Bible, Rabbinics, Hebrew, Judaic history—all of that every day, along with math, science, and history. We had a meeting with other youth groups, and I was one of the only girls leading anything the whole Saturday.

In the Orthodox movement, girls and women are not supposed to lead. It's this concept called *kol isha* that translates to "the voice of a woman." When men are in this spirituality zone, they don't want to listen to women's voices because it might sexually arouse them and throw them off course from praying. So girls don't usually sing in public.

In a synagogue, there's a *mehitzah*, or line or wall, that separates men and women. It can be a row of plants or a curtain. The more observant you are, the higher the wall gets.

Why Do You Want to Be Counted for Minyan?

Darcy, 23
Jewish (Modern Orthodox)

I'm Modern Orthodox. I keep kosher, keep Shabbos, keep all the holidays. I don't wear very revealing clothes, but I do show some skin. In some ways, I agree with covering more skin. But at the same time, my logic is basically: It's probably better if I did, but I don't really feel like it, and I'm not at that point yet, so I'm not going to bother. I wear pants, I don't cover my arms, I don't plan on covering my hair all the time when I get married.

I disagree with the rule against wearing pants, because for centuries religious Jewish women wore pants, particularly in the Ottoman Empire. Pants were considered more modest than skirts because if the wind blows, your skirt might blow up. If you wear them loose, pants don't show anything. Why are you trying to pretend that you don't have legs? We aren't like the Victorians, who put little skirts around piano legs, lest you get aroused at the thought that the piano had legs like a woman.

Judaism is very big on understanding that people are at different places at different times and you should always be climbing up, growing spiritually. You shouldn't be going down. But just because I'm not at the top does not make me a bad person. Different people are ready for different things—to accept different obligations—at different times. There's some understanding of personal preference.

On the role of women—I think any liberal-thinking Orthodox at some point does have issues. I got over the problems I had. I did some more study to understand the logic behind what appears to be discrimination against women and realized that it isn't at all—it's actually the reverse.

Now I end up explaining this to a lot of women who come to the synagogue. I go to a synagogue downtown during the day to say Kaddish. Women come in, and they're all upset. They say, "It's terrible. They don't count women for minyan. And they don't let women do this and that." I'm like, "It's not terrible. Here's why it's a good thing. . . . "

It's not an issue for me, personally. Part of the reason is that there's a view in more religious circles that women are superior and closer to G-d and more naturally spiritual. Women are exempt from synagogue and most time-bound commandments, except for things like Shabbos. Women can make up their own prayers. They can pray whenever they want because women are closer to G-d already.

Men, on the other hand, are more attached to the material world and more involved in business life and secular life. So it's harder for them to connect to G-d. So they're required to go to synagogue, and they're required to meet with ten other men to pray. Women are exempt from that, because in a way we're better.

If they counted women for a minyan, then women would be obligated to go to make up the minyan. I personally would rather not have that obligation. Why do you want to be counted for minyan?

Are women and men just different? Religiously observant women of all three faiths thought so. These differences justified the treatment of women and the division of labor between the sexes. You'll find Mari's argument that "God made us different" echoed by Christian and Jewish women later in this chapter.

God Made Us Different

Mari,* 21
Muslim
*not her real name

The separation of the men and women for prayers is because we don't want the men leering. It's for protection of our bodies. That's why we cover. I wear skirts, long sleeves. It's debatable if you can show your feet or not—there's different schools of thought on that in Islam.

In the summer, it's hard to find long sleeves that cover your arms and are not very tight and that are long enough. Most of the clothes nowadays are shorter, tighter, and see-through. We can buy those clothes and save them for the parties that we have. We have sisters' parties, all-sisters gatherings. We dress up for each other. We wear what we can't normally wear—like those miniskirts we want, or those tank tops. We can show our hair to each other. We dress up and fix our hair. We can only wear these things with each other.

I was very feministic before. I used to believe that we were better than the guys. We should have the opportunity to have a career, and both people should care for the kids. Then I changed my mind, because I realized that in Islam, in the eyes of God, we were equal. No one should be above the other. But then I realize that God made us different. We're more nurturing, more emotional, than the guys. Guys can be nurturing, too, but they are more hard-core breadwinners.

It is mostly cultural—the girls stay home and take care of the kids. They don't work. But I still think that guys should also help out. Nowadays girls work, too, they have their own careers.

My whole focus right now is that education's most important. We've always been taught that you have to seek knowledge from the cradle to the grave—that's from the Prophet's (peace be upon him) words. Because without knowledge, you don't understand what God's words are, you don't understand what you're reading.

It's important for a girl to have education because we're the ones who raise the kids. We have to teach the kids Islamic knowledge and any kind of knowledge, and they have to go out in the society when they grow up. We make the people who you see.

One of the people who had the strongest views about religion is Kara. She believes that all religions—Christianity, Judaism, Islam, and others—perpetuate the oppression of women around the world.

Women Take a Subservient Role

Kara, 23
Atheist

I don't know any religions that have been terribly good for women. When I think of religion, I usually think of Christianity first, then Judaism, and then maybe Muslims as an afterthought. In all of them, women take a subservient role as possessions of the men, as opposed to being equal human beings.

A lot of times, when they talk about "man" in the Bible or in the Qur'an or whatever, they're talking about men. Sometimes now we'll interpret it as "human," but I think what they're really talking about is men.

And the roles that women take in those stories, like in stories of the Bible—women are pawns in the men's games. I'm thinking of the story of Ruth and Naomi. As far as I know, Ruth is Naomi's daughter-in-law. She's faithful and loyal to Naomi, and that was a good thing.

But I remember studying in a class about the role that Ruth takes on in the story. The way she remains faithful and the way she helps Naomi out is by getting married, and lying with this rich man, and being a servant, and being totally submissive. The way she is successful in life is by capturing a rich man—or, really, being captured by a rich man.

There are roles for women in the Bible and in other religions, but the whole idea behind lots of religions is just this subservience and this belief in a higher power that I don't think exists. And I don't think that that kind of thinking unleashes people's creativity and their willingness to change and be masters of society.

Most of the young women I interviewed were either in college or collegebound. Their goals included careers as pharmacist, psychologist, educator, politician, and diplomat, to name a few. They didn't anticipate that their gender would limit their educational and professional opportunities. Several generations ago, women did not have these choices.

As society has changed, religious institutions and traditions have been pressured to change also. Women and girls have won new opportunities. For example, in many Catholic churches, the term altar server replaced altar boy; girls serve beside boys. Women pastors and rabbis lead churches and synagogues.

But changes such as these in religious traditions that are thousands of years old are not without controversy. Some people believe that religious institutions have gone too far. Others believe they haven't gone far enough. Two of the young women I interviewed expressed these opposing stances.

Women Shouldn't Be Up There Speaking

Ilene, 18
Christian (born again)

There are some people who believe that women should be allowed to minister in the church. But from what I've read and from what I've studied, women aren't allowed to minister. The Bible says that during the service women shouldn't be up there speaking—men should be leading in that role.

I think that men and women just have different roles in God's creation. I don't believe that women should be ministers, because I've found it written in God's word that women shouldn't be the ones leading the men because men were created first. It says it in Genesis, chapter 2, where it talks about how God created man and then put him in the Garden of Eden. God saw that man needed a companion. He put Adam to sleep, and he took out one of Adam's ribs. And out of that he created the woman.

Women should just be the listeners. The Bible doesn't say anything against women teaching. Women should be allowed to teach, but not teach men. They should teach women or people younger than them. God's just given them a different role than men.

Some people think there's a problem with women working if they have a family. It's understandable if you need the money, but I think God will provide. If I have a family, it's my responsibility to stop working and stay home with my kids because that's the role God's given women.

When you have children, it's your role to take care of them and to raise them up to be godly men and women willing to serve God and to live their lives for him. There's a chapter in Proverbs 31. It says that the woman should be diligent in her work, work with her hands, and take care of her family, and just be that godly woman that he desires for us to be.

There Were Strong Women in the Bible

Hesed, 14
Christian (United Methodist)

My mother is now at a church in Melrose Park. She's pastor there.

Southern Baptists don't allow women to be preachers. And Paul does say that men should be the initiators—a lot of people think he's a woman-hater. You have to understand that in those times women were like property and treated like dogs. And I think as time changes, you have to apply a more modern context to the Bible.

I believe that if Jesus didn't want women to be leaders, he wouldn't have entrusted so many key actions and key occurrences in Bible history to them. Mary Magdalene was the first person who saw him when he rose from the dead, and he gave her that task to go and tell the apostles that he was alive. He could have chosen a man for that, but he chose a woman. God chose to bear a son through a woman when he could have just created one.

There were strong women in the Bible—Esther was a queen, and she used her position for God's glory and saved her people.

I don't think that there is anything in the Bible that says women shouldn't be leaders or women shouldn't be equal to men. I think a lot of the church— where it is today—is the result of women's leadership.

Can an Orthodox Jewish woman be a feminist? Miriam tells why she's chosen to remain in the Orthodox movement although she dislikes many of the establishment's views on women's issues.

I Don't Feel That I Need to Go Looking for a Perfect Community

Miriam, 22
Jewish (Orthodox)

Should I wear skirts, or should I not wear skirts? That was never the focus of all my religious angst. I realize that for some people it's really annoying to wear skirts, but it doesn't bother me.

For some people I know, pants become a weird symbol, because it's the demarcation between the more right-wing Orthodox and the more modern Orthodox. The right-wing Orthodox would never dream of wearing pants. It's a sign of women's liberation. Wearing pants becomes a big statement. Everyone makes assumptions about you.

The dress code, as I see it, is skirts below the knee, and sleeves below the elbow or to the elbow, and necklines that aren't too low. You can look nice, but it shouldn't matter to you to look fabulous or to look really sexy. In general, it's sort of a judgment call.

And ultimately, in the society we live in now, I don't know that it matters if someone looks at your lower arm and thinks it's sexy. There's a certain idea that you can remove sexuality from all interactions that I don't think is true. I think that even though Orthodoxy is pretty restrictive in what women wear, there is that recognition that we don't have to cover everything.

I think this sets sort of a baseline for what is accepted in the public realm and what's not.

Who Is Responsible, Men or Women?

It's a big question as to what extent women are responsible for the way men look at them. We are told men can't control themselves, so you have to cover yourself so they don't have to control themselves. But there are a lot of men who can control themselves. So on the one hand, you're doing this as a favor to men and the moral standing of the world. Then there's the aspect that you're doing this for yourself, given the fact that men are going to look at you in a certain way and you shouldn't think of yourself as a sexual object.

Orthodox Judaism is a gender-segregated society, essentially. Among the most rigorously Orthodox—or whatever you want to call them—men and women are in essentially two different worlds. And the way they're segregated is according to which commandments you fulfill and don't fulfill.

Like, men are obligated to fulfill the mitzvah, the commandment of learning Torah, and women aren't. But there's all sorts of other stuff that goes with that, like that means that men spend more time at *shul* or yeshiva with other men, whereas women spend more time at home with their children. Or in a lot of circles, that means that women aren't allowed to learn Talmud. It introduces a power dynamic in the relationship in the sense that the husband is the figure who knows the law. He's the authority.

There's a lot of social prejudice against things that seem to be too inclusive of women, even in a community like this, a liberal university. We'll be in a room, and there will be two women and eight men—you have to wait for ten men to start services. And someone would say, "There are only eight people here." When I first got here, I'd go crazy. I was like, "What do you mean? There are 10 people now!" Now, all I say is, "There are eight men," and they sort of figure it out.

When I first got here, I was much more militant about being feminist. I felt like everyone had to agree with me, and so I used to pester people. Now everyone knows where I stand. They think, "She's right—marriage is a really problematic institution, especially the way it's constructed in the Jewish texts." Or they think, "She's crazy."

I sort of feel like my job is to be the wake-up call for a lot of people. I definitely know a lot of Orthodox men who never thought about things in a certain way. It's not that they think that the subjugation of women is OK, but they just think, "We know what's better for them than they do." It's very patronizing. Like no one's pointed out to them that they're patronizing. And I don't necessarily want them to stop being Orthodox, but I want these things to be problematized for them, and for them to at least understand why they are problems for me.

Feminist—it's always a loaded word. I feel like it describes a liberal perspective of treating people as individuals regardless of a whole list of things, and also of sensitivity to issues of gender in whatever society you're in. I do identify as a feminist because I participate in that kind of critique, even if I don't necessarily adopt all the conclusions for myself. I'm still sort of working through what I think of gender differentiation in the context of religious law.

It's not like there aren't issues of power in the traditional Jewish home in terms of the fact that women are much less educated. They are also less educated in terms of their critical thinking, not just in terms of actual content. Those are big problems for me. But I don't think that the ideal solution is to make women like men. There are a lot of things that I think the traditional male education is lacking.

The problems with Orthodoxy are that it has these very rigid rules in which a lot of things are proscribed, especially for women. But it's not entirely negative; it works for a lot of people. Not counting often goes with being exempt. So, for example, women may have more options for how to spend their time, like they can stay home and read or play with their kids while their husband has to go to shul.

Also, there's a lot about Orthodox Jewish life that doesn't take place in the synagogue. And buying into the idea that the minyan is the most important thing, buys into the idea that Orthodox Judaism does take place in the synagogue. I don't really think that's true. It has a lot to do with what happens during the Friday-night dinner. I think traditional orthodoxy has created a society in which family is more important to men than it is in a lot of American society, which is a good thing for women and people in general.

Also, I don't feel that the question of women has been decided in secular America. In liberal academia, you say "family," and everyone's like, "She's probably anti-abortion." It gets reduced to this very simple binary of pro-family equals anti-woman. And that's not actually true.

A lot of people, who are working more with people than with theory, will be like, "Pro-family is pro-women." For them, family is very essential to women. I don't know if family is more or less essential to women than men, but it's been very useful for me to have my foot in two places on the feminist issue, as opposed to just in one place. I can see the good things that can come out of traditional society. I think that puts you in a better position to criticize and to improve on it.

I once studied with a girl who was thinking about converting to Judaism and she was having a lot of issues with the role of women in Orthodoxy. She was like, "How do you deal with it?" And basically my answer was that there are some things that are more important to me than other things. But I can't convince someone else why they should have the same priorities.

Do I want to identify as Orthodox, when the so-called Orthodox establishment has all these opinions that I don't like, like about women's issues? I think it's not viable for me to be non-Orthodox. I'd rather be in a community where, despite all of these problems, I can read a piece of Talmud and there will be others in the shul who I can talk to about it, than be in a community where everyone's egalitarian but no one knows the meaning of what they're saying. So in terms of what community I'll be affiliated with, to the extent that I'll be affiliated with anyone, they have to be educated and they have to be committed.

For most Jews in America who have any Jewish education, it ends when they're thirteen—and then what? What happens on their Friday-night dinner is what happens at any other dinner—but then they're still Jewish because they went to synagogue, they're eating a certain kind of food, and they didn't cook it on Shabbos, and that kind of stuff.

But there's something very important to me, for example, about a family where on Friday-night dinner all the kids say what they learned in yeshiva that week, where the idea of study and practice are carried out throughout the normal parts of life as well.

Academic discourse is like scholarship for scholarship's sake, whereas what you study in a Jewish context is scholarship where scholarship has all these other meanings—scholarship is an act of service to God, scholarship is a way of improving yourself, scholarship is a way to improve the world, and scholarship is how you become part of the religious establishment. You leave your mark through educating yourself and educating others. It's questionable to what extent women can be part of the religious establishment, even today.

Learning Torah

I'm very attached to learning Torah. I went to a yeshiva for women for a year. They have a heavy emphasis on Talmud, which is allegedly the most controversial thing for women to learn.

I guess in some ways, my model of personal success as a Jew was adapted from the traditional exclusively male model of studying and being knowledgeable about these texts. Most of my role models are male, which has been an issue because the career path open to them is very different from what's open to me.

The truth is that a lot of my male cousins and their children, from when they were three, they had an apparatus to make them into real scholars in a way that I probably will never be. There's this whole population of men who know a lot, and who study all the time in a way that I don't. I've almost lost the race just by that. But I think there are things I can bring to it that they can't—a certain kind of critical thinking, or being able to speak to a certain audience.

Now women study Talmud, but there aren't any women of the caliber of the mid-level men. I have a few female role models who are breaking ground in terms of how you read text or how you think about things, Jewish philosophy.

I'd like to come up with ideas, or ways of reading Jewish texts, that shape a lot of people. I'd have to study for many more years. I might just want to teach high school—that would be fun too.

I enjoy being around people who feel like their life has a purpose—they know what they want and what they want for their children. This isn't specific to my community at all. But it just happens that I've found a community in which there are a lot of really sincere and devoted people who do a really good job raising good people for children. And I like that. I don't feel that I need to go looking for a perfect community.

I Don't Worship with Some Guy in Rome

A devout Catholic, and a lesbian, Karla explains why she's chosen to remain in the Catholic faith despite the church's condemnation of her lifestyle.

Karla, 23
Christian (Catholic)

I grew up in Trinidad, in the Caribbean. It's maybe 80 percent Catholic—not only Catholic, but fundamentalist Catholic. So I grew up in an environment where I went to church at least three times a week, including 6:00 in the morning before school.

I went to fourteen years of Catholic school in Trinidad before I came to college here. In Trinidad there is no concept of separation of church and state, so public schools are free and they are Catholic. We celebrated all the Catholic holidays and had special masses within school time. There was a chapel on the premises of the school and a convent.

I had the first communion at seven. I took my confirmation at fourteen. Then I taught confirmation for two years after that. I got involved a lot in school in organizing the students to say the rosary at lunchtime, leading prayer, things like that. I went to confession every week. I would describe myself as a Catholic overachiever back then.

I went to college in a small town in Mississippi. I came to a church that could fit maybe one hundred and fifty people. In Trinidad, I went to a church that could fit a thousand people at each mass. What I found in Mississippi was more of a sense of community.

A lot of Catholic churches are run as less a community and as more of "you and your connection to God." You're encouraged to do what you think will please God—spending five hours in church, a lot of kneeling and praying and kneeling and praying—and very little doing. It was a pretty affluent congregation in Trinidad. There was very little community service toward a ghetto that was right in our backyard or very little "Let's help somebody else." But we'd sit

MY FAITH JOURNEY

and kneel and be in church as often as possible. So in that sense, it was more "me and God" versus "me and God's people." You went to church, you talked to God, you went home. I kneel, I stand, I kneel, I stand.

I went to church as many times a week as I could, thinking that would make me a good Catholic. I spent lots of time in the chapel thinking that would please God and that would make me a good Catholic. And I said the rosary often—that would please God and that would make me a good Catholic.

So getting to college, I got involved in social justice through Corpus Christi, which is a Catholic social-justice group. There was a social hour after church, which is something I'd never experienced before. We discussed issues, we did things. My vision of the church changed from sitting and praying to getting up and doing—and I recognized that as a way to please some higher power.

Coming Out

Around my freshman year of college, I came out as a lesbian. Being an overachieving Catholic and then getting that on top of it—it was a hard, harsh crash. I had blinders on about my sexual orientation for a long while. One day I got up and I was like, "Oh." I went to the church. I sat there in the back of the church, and I just cried for five hours straight. And the next day I got back up and I was like, "OK, I'm going to deal." And I was fine.

As a child, I don't think I ever heard anybody say, "You're going to go to hell if you're gay." And within my family, there were never any negative connotations about gay people. But in general, you know that it's against Church teachings. I know many people who heard the priest say, "It's a great sin against God to be a homosexual."

I kept going to church. But slowly but surely the Catholic guilt crept in. I stopped going to church for maybe eight months. Something in me was seeing my sexual orientation, and the fact that I was in a relationship, as a mortal sin.

Growing up, I was taught the difference between a mortal sin and a venal sin. A venal sin is something petty: I lied, I was mean to this person. In the Catholic Church, anything that's serious, you consider that a mortal sin. The teaching is that if you die with a mortal sin on your soul, there's no guarantee that you'll go to heaven.

I came back after summer break, and I started going to church again. But I wouldn't receive communion. The teaching is if you have a mortal sin on your soul, you can't receive communion until you take confession. I didn't see the point in going to confession and confessing it every week without any plan to change.

"Take It."

One day I was in mass. There were maybe twelve people and the priest. I didn't go up for communion, and the priest came to me and said, "Take it." I guess he was telling me that whatever I think I did that was so bad—it was not so bad. After that, I went and spoke to him about it. This was the second priest that I came out to. I had talked to a priest in Trinidad.

The priest in college pretty much told me the same thing—to forget what the Church is teaching you and that you are who you are in terms of what you do, how you treat others, and not who you sleep with. After that, I felt more welcome in that community. I participated heavily in church. I did the readings at mass. I took communion. I taught Sunday school. By my last year of college, I was vice president of the Catholic Students Association and the treasurer of the Gay, Lesbian, Bisexual Association on campus. I found myself in a community that accepted me for who I was. I felt very comfortable being Catholic and being a lesbian at that point in time.

I Missed the Structure

I left college and went to Maine for a while and started going to a Catholic church again. The congregation was so big, there was no sense of community. I started going to the UU church, Unitarian Universalist. We had a female pastor, which is the first time I had ever experienced a woman as a church leader. She was wonderful.

There was a social hour after. I really enjoyed the community there. It was a church that welcomed the GLBT [Gay, Lesbian, Bisexual, Transgender] community. It's a very open kind of church. This reinforced the idea that church is community.

I did miss the traditions of the Catholic Church. There's something celestial about walking into an ornate Catholic church, a cathedral-like building. In the olden days, they thought they had to make everything pretty for God—the high ceilings, the glass windows, and the tall high pillars on the altar. There is that sensation you get when you walk in. It's like, "Ah." You just get that

MY FAITH JOURNEY

feeling—I guess you could say it's a presence of God or the presence of some kind of spirit. I missed that. It's so different from walking into a twentieth-century church. A lot of the new churches are just brick and mortar.

I missed the structure, I guess. I could say a mass by heart. I could start rattling it off—exactly what the priest is saying. The UU church is so much less structured. If you feel like speaking and sharing, you just did.

Then I moved to Indiana. I found a UU church there, but I didn't get the same feeling I got in Maine—again reinforcing to me that it's all about the people in the community and not the church itself, or the religion, or the structure. The pastor again was a woman and didn't know how to preach. The people were friendly, but it's an instinctual feeling sometimes—either you mesh or you don't mesh.

I was commuting between Indiana and Chicago because my partner lived in Chicago. There are two GLBT Catholic organizations in Chicago. There's one called AGLO [Archdiocese Gay and Lesbian Outreach]. It's a group within the confines of the diocese that has a mass especially for GLBT people. It's held at a Catholic church and under the guidelines of the Catholic Church and Cardinal George.

Dignity

In 1997 the pope wrote a letter saying that people can be born with genes that make them homosexual. That was a big switch for the Church. Before that, he was saying it was a choice, and you should choose not to be that way. They were no longer condemning the homosexual; they were condemning homosexual acts. In a nutshell, the pope said, "You need to bear this as your cross that Jesus has given you and just not act on it." The Church was teaching that it's OK for you to be homosexual, but you can't be in a relationship. This is a teaching that AGLO runs under. These are the bylaws that they have to agree to, and technically teach, to continue to meet in a Catholic church.

When I moved to Chicago two years ago, I started to go to Dignity. Dignity is a nationwide organization that recognizes the holiness in all relationships, in all genders, including intersexed—this means having more than one genitalia—and bigender, people who consider themselves both male and female, et cetera. We don't have a priest assigned to us because we are not meeting under the guidelines of the Catholic Church. All our priests are volunteers. If it were known that they were holding mass for us, or marrying us, they would be in serious trouble.

Dignity used to meet under the Catholic Church. But as the Catholic teachings became more explicit, Dignity was told that we couldn't perform unions and in any way promote relationships between two people of the same sex. Dignity could not adhere to what they were saying. They made the decision to leave the Catholic Church and meet outside the realm of the diocese. We meet at a Methodist Church right now.

At my church, we're very gender sensitive. We do not acknowledge God as male. So when we say what is known as the "Our Father," we say "Our Maker."

We try to take out all use of "he" from the mass. Sometimes we use songs that have "king" in it, or "he" or "his." We don't say "king" or "queen," we say "reign." Instead of "thy kingdom come," we say, "thy reign come."

"In the name of the Father, Son, and the Holy Spirit"—we use "In the name of the Maker, Redeemer, and the Life-giving Spirit."

So we've made it very gender-inclusive, acknowledging that we are all made in the image and likeness of God. So it's not male or female. I very much appreciate the fact that it is practiced that way.

The Pope

Canada just OK'd gay marriages, and right now there's an immigration law in Congress that would allow an American to sponsor a same-sex partner of a different nation for a green card.

The pope put out a cry to Catholic and non-Catholic persons and politicians saying that it is in the interest of society not to give any kind of institution to two people of the same sex. He beseeched Catholic politicians to not allow any kind of political sanctioning of marriage between same-sex people. His general statement was that two people in a same-sex relationship is wrong—marriage is between a man and a woman. He spoke of putting children in a household with two people of the same sex as equivalent to doing violence to that child. That's a statement that's causing a huge uproar.

To think that two human beings who love a child are somehow doing violence to that child because they are the same sex is just preposterous to me. But to me, the statement was no surprise. One of the goals of Dignity is to somehow reunite Dignity to the Catholic Church, to change the views of the Catholic Church to accept homosexuality. I personally think it's a pipe dream.

There are some people you just don't argue with because you just aren't going to change their minds. I have no illusion that this pope, or the next pope, or even the next pope after that, is going to listen up anytime soon.

Some people very much need and want to be accepted by the official Catholic Church someday. That need and desire are not there for me. Again, it's all about the community and the people I worship with. I don't worship with some guy in Rome. I don't worship with Cardinal George in his cathedral. I worship with fifty people at my church.

If someone were to ask me if I was part of the Catholic Church, I'd have to say yes and no. I consider myself Catholic—whether anyone else does, that's up to them. I know Cardinal George wouldn't, the pope wouldn't. But I practice in the Catholic tradition, and I also believe that just because somebody, humans, have named this person the head of the church, he's not the head of my church. I don't see that one person has the right to call the shots for the rest of the world on how they run their spirituality and what guidelines they use. It's not as if we haven't had any corrupt popes before.

It's a combination of picking and choosing. I like the tradition of Catholicism. I grew up in this. I feel comfortable here. But these are the things I don't like, so I disregard those. So with rules and regulations—I acknowledge the ones I want to acknowledge. The ones that I think are stupid and dumb, I'm going to break them if I don't think it hurts anybody for me to do so.

I'm no longer grounded in the institution of religion. So I call myself Catholic because, if I had to give myself a label, that is the closest word to describe my method of practicing my spirituality. I practice in the Catholic tradition. The masses I go to are held in the Catholic tradition. I enjoy the Catholic tradition. I grew up in it. It's part of me.

But spirituality, for me, is more about the community, the people I worship with—not only worship with, but act with. I've gotten away from saying the rosary or saying my prayers before I go to sleep at night to going to work at soup kitchens or going to serve people in another way. And I think I can affect better change that way.

Many Faiths, One World

Many of the people who contributed to this book marveled at the power of religion to bring out the best in people. The principle "love thy neighbor" can be found in the teachings of all faiths. But clearly this axiom is often not followed.

During some of my conversations, people mentioned bloody conflicts around the globe that involve religious differences—in places such as the Middle East, Chechnya, the Balkans, and Kashmir. They also discussed clashes among people within their own faith— especially between fundamentalists and moderates. You'll hear from a few of these people in this chapter.

You'll also hear from young people who see a role for themselves in bridging religious differences. Their viewpoints are wide ranging. They include a young man who is studying to be an overseas missionary so he can convert non-Christians to his beliefs. Others are working toward increasing understanding and cooperation between people of different faiths around the world.

They Have to Know the Love of Jesus

Evan, 21
Christian (Evangelical)

I'm studying to be a missionary overseas in closed countries, like China, North Korea, or Saudi Arabia. Closed countries are places where it's hard for Christians to get in and help people. I want to go to places where most Christians won't go because of fear.

As a missionary, I will not force my doctrine down anyone's throat. I will go and serve, and even die, so that sinful people may see the love of Christ displayed through me. When they have seen Jesus in me and have heard the truth of him, some people will be irresistibly drawn to know him. I am going overseas to help them in their needs, but more than that, I am going to give them Jesus Christ, who will ultimately satisfy the longing of their hearts.

The aim of the Christian should be ultimate love for another. And that ultimate love is only found in sharing the unconditional love of Jesus Christ. Jesus Christ is the only name by which a person may be saved. Therefore, if I truly loved people, I would not keep silent. Rather, I would share the truth and reality of Jesus Christ. Even if they hate me for it, I must tell them. They have to know the love of Jesus.

Some would ask if it is dangerous. My reply is, "Absolutely." Christians are hated for their faith. However, it is in the times of martyrdom and suffering that Christ prevails through his people. Christians are not called to lives of comfort and wealth. Christians are called to give up all security and self-sufficiency and to lay down their lives for the sake of the Gospel. Since Christ died and suffered to give me life, how can I not die and suffer for others so that they, too, might know this life in Christ?

When Christ calls a man to follow him, Christ calls him to come and die. "For me to live is Christ and to die is gain."[32] "But I do not consider my life of any account as dear to myself, so that I may finish my course and the ministry which I received from the Lord Jesus, to testify solemnly of the gospel for the grace of God."[33]

Currently, I minister to male and female prostitutes from 10 P.M. to 3 A.M. on Friday and Saturday nights here in Chicago. I take them out for coffee or just talk

---

[32] Philippians 1:21
[33] Acts 20:24

with them. I try to get them to the ministry center I represent in order to give them a change of clothes, to get AIDS testing, and to be taught from the Bible. I try to get them off the streets and off drugs. Only Jesus can heal their hearts.

This ministry with prostitutes stretches me in numerous ways. I cannot love these prostitutes on my own. I must have the love of Christ flowing through me in order to effectively love these people.

The same applies to my overseas work. In and of myself, I cannot unconditionally love people. I must be connected with Christ in order to truly love people. I am going to be serving in the Middle East as a missionary, and there is no way I alone can love Muslims who so passionately hate me and my faith. But the love of Jesus controls me and enables me to love them despite their hatred for me. I would gladly be martyred or tortured if that meant that even a few would come to know Jesus.

Fundamentalists Got It All Wrong

Oz, 20
Muslim

Some religions are more successful because they are more open to others and accepting. But then there are many people who are less accepting of other beliefs. I think these are two forces that are struggling to get control. There is a struggle between fundamentalism and the secular movement everywhere in the world in all religions.

It's a struggle that, unless there is a big revolution for their side, is doomed for the fundamentalists because their opposition is united across the world.

There is not much of a difference between a secular Muslim and a secular Christian. But there is a huge difference between a fundamentalist Christian and a fundamentalist Muslim.

That's why there is this—you might want to call it—world religion. It's a mixture of everything. My beliefs encompass some Eastern self-centered beliefs. For example, I believe that there's a god in me, and that this belief drives me to do better things. You can't call it strictly Muslim, although there have been sects of Islam that claim this.

There's a hint of Eastern religions everywhere. It's not as obvious as fundamentalist religions—it doesn't say, "Here are our beliefs. Repent and believe or go to hell." It's very subtle. Like you read a book about success, and there are a lot of hints in there about how you tap your inner power. It's a way of living. There's a subtle message in our global society that if you do certain things, believe in certain very open, interpretable things, then you will be successful and be happy. It's the global religion.

I think it's the ultimate end of this whole religious quest. You can trace this back to just simple interaction of societies. We started as very small, different, separated societies. You had all these gods and different ideas of morality and of what's good and what's bad. Then the monotheistic religions made a bigger union of morality, and now there's even a bigger union currently in motion. We're coming together by making sure that our morals match, because societies cannot live in peace when they have huge differences in morality. So they're slowly unifying their morality.

I'm a Muslim. I want to claim ownership of my religion, too. Throughout all of this speech, I might have sounded like there is Islam and there is my version of it. I fully believe that my version is right. I think what I'm doing is Islam.

People who are fundamentalists got it all wrong. That's just my view. They're not going to be successful in this world because of the obvious reason that they're divided and we're united. And although there is no obvious physical fight, if you can call this a war, I think the secular people are on the defense. But still as more people stop traditional practices, I think the other side tries twice as hard to bring them forward again.

The Israeli-Palestinian conflict was on the minds of many of the Jews I interviewed. In the summer of 2003, a number of them traveled to Israel for summer youth programs, internships, or college. On the following pages, several Jews and a Palestinian Muslim share their views about the conflict.

Their Hands Are Tied

Darcy, 23
Jewish (Modern Orthodox)

There are professors at the University of Chicago who are anti-Semitic, including a few Jewish ones. We say there's no anti-Semite like a self-hating Jew. I had professors who would talk about the poor, innocent Palestinians who were sitting there on the land until the Jews came and massacred them. It's not exactly true.

Historically, the Palestinians are a bunch of refugees from a bunch of different Arab countries who got kicked out of their own countries. They're a mixture of Syrian, Lebanese, Jordanian, et cetera—there is no "Palestinian people," as a distinct group. They're from all over. None of the Arab countries are making any effort to offer them asylum. If Israel kicked the Palestinians out, who's going to take them? Nobody wants them.

I will be one of the first people to say it's not black and white. It's not that Palestinians are bad and Jews are good. It's not that Palestinians are good and Jews are bad. Both are at fault. At the same time, I don't think there's very much the Israeli government can do; their hands are tied. And they are tied even more by the world.

When September 11 happened in America, it was OK for America to go to war and take out two entire countries. The world complained and fussed, but it was OK. When there's a suicide bombing in Israel daily and the Israeli government puts up a roadblock, "Oh, my G-d, it's terrible." And the entire world comes down en mass with wrath and fury on Israel's head, which is grossly unfair, very hypocritical. If it were any country other than Israel, nobody would say anything. Israel is like the role model for the world, and they have to be perfect, which is hard for anyone to live up to.

Yes, I think it's OK to find fault with things the Israeli government is doing. But it annoys me when people don't do their research and don't have their facts straight and then start complaining. In that case, I think it's generally better to not say anything.

You Try Having Nothing to Live For

Sara, 18
Jewish (Reform)

I love Israel. I love the place and the people there. One thing that separates me from a lot of Jewish kids I know is that I really hate the Israeli government. They are ruining everything. I'm really against the occupation of Palestine. I'm not sure I see a clear solution right now. But I think that bulldozing people's homes and ripping out their way of life, like their olive trees, isn't going to solve much. It just causes more animosity.

In February or the beginning of March, NFTY [North American Federation of Temple Youth] had this huge national convention in Washington, D.C. One of the workshops that we had was about Israel. Most of the kids in there were like, "Why are the Palestinians doing all of these horrible things?" "They're horrible, and they're just bad people."

And I'm like, "They're not just doing this for fun. Don't tell me they're doing it just because they're bad people. You try having nothing to live for." And I found myself in yelling matches with people. Actually, I only shouted at someone once because they were getting really obnoxious.

I don't condone suicide bombing. That's a horrible thing, too, that's not getting them anywhere. But we have to realize that there's a reason for it and until that reason is taken away it will continue to happen. It happens because people are living in squalor and they have very little. Terrorist organizations will come and say, "If you do this, you'll have a place in heaven and we'll take care of your family. We'll make sure they have food and shelter." And if a man can't give that to his family, he'll be willing to go to extreme lengths to get that for them.

As liberal as the Reform movement is, they still want us to love Israel. And a lot of rabbis feel that if they teach that what Israel is doing is bad, we won't love Israel as much. I really admire our rabbis—we have two of them, we have a woman and a male rabbi at my synagogue. Both of them have been fairly outspoken against what Israel is doing. But there are a lot of rabbis that aren't. And there's a lot of people in every movement of Judaism who are like, "Well, they're just trying to defend themselves. They're doing whatever is best for the people." And I really don't think they are.

It was really weird for people to hear that from someone like me. Everyone knows I love Israel a lot. But I also realize that the government is really screwing up right now.

A lot of it is misinformation. I don't get most of my information from mainstream media. I don't even watch TV, because it's obviously not the whole truth. Israeli news tends to be less biased than American news. There's an Israeli newspaper. They have an English Web site called *Haaretzdaily*. They are probably the least biased newspaper I can find. They'll publish articles about the horrible things that Israel is doing, the horrible things the Palestinians are doing.

I like reading Web sites—the Palestinian news sources—just because they give me a different viewpoint. I mean, both sides obviously still have a bias so you have to read between the lines to see who's telling the truth and figure things out. But I feel like I have a better picture of the truth than if I just read the *Tribune* or something.

I'm going to college in Washington, D.C. I'll study international relations. After college, I think I want to join a small organization that will send me off to random countries so I can help. I want to be one of those people who can speak five or six languages. I understand a lot of Hebrew. I want to learn Arabic.

I will be in Israel next year. I'm deferring from college for the year. There's a kibbutz I will stay on. They have an intensive Hebrew program. I will learn to speak Hebrew fluently. I will also work with the Red Jewish Star. It's the equivalent of the Red Cross in Israel. You learn CPR, and you go out on the ambulances on emergency calls. My mom is worried about the violence there, or that I'll go and decide I don't want to come home.

You Have Two Types of People

Haron, 20
Muslim

I'm a first-generation American. My family is from a small village between Ramallah and Jerusalem. On one side of the village are Jewish settlements—it hurts me every time I look that way and know that that used to be one of my relatives' farmland. I've been back home a couple of times—the last time was in '98.

I have a lot of family there. My family talks to them every week. It's not as bad as other areas. such as Gaza, such as Jericho, such as Nablus, such as Jerusalem. But you are not able to be as free. The whole country feels it. They still feel the curfews, the struggles.

My grandmother is not allowed to go sell any more fruits. That was her job. She would go to Jerusalem and sell the fruit she picked in the morning, at the doors of Jerusalem. My grandfather is not allowed to go to the factory anymore because the Jewish soldiers won't let him leave the village. Since they were teens, my uncles have had a curfew where they have to be home before eight o'clock or before nightfall.

We are far away in distance, but my heart is with them. So it does hurt a lot when I see Palestinian children cry on TV and when I listen to stories my grandparents tell me about what is happening back home—mothers seeing their little kids pass away in front of them, or little kids seeing that their fathers are in jail. I feel for them.

Everyone asks the same thing—is the fighting based on religious or national freedom? To tell you the truth, it's both. There are Palestinian people fighting because Jerusalem is the third holiest site in Muslim beliefs. So people are fighting for that land. Then there are others who are fighting because they want their land back.

Many of my friends are always asking me what's going on, because they know that the media doesn't portray it correctly. I tell them. They'll put it together and say, "You're right. What they're saying about how the Palestinians are killing more Jews doesn't make any sense. They've only got stones, and the soldiers have their rockets, tanks, and their guns." So the media portrays it incorrectly. Every group has their extremists—Christians, Jews, Muslims. I don't like how they depict Muslims as one, as terrorists.

The American people want to see the truth. It's all media that doesn't show the one hundred percent truth. So the American people are confused as to how to look at the situation. They don't show both sides of the story. Usually when you hear a story on the Israeli side, it's front-page news. But when you see one on the Palestinian side, it's usually in the back. You actually have to look for it.

Ever since the second *intifada* started, a few Jews in this country have been more considerate toward the Palestinians. And then there are others who have been more harsh. To me there are two types of Jews—the ones who care for the Palestinians and don't like what's happening back home and the ones who actually approve of it. In every other religion, you have two types of people. So that's how I look at the Jews right now, as two types of people—the ones I can talk to and the ones I can't stand.

We Need to Explore New Horizons

Kamran, 21
Muslim

Both my parents are from India, but I was born here. I lived my whole life here. We were fairly religious. I was given a thorough secular, as well as religious, education. And I've studied a lot with scholars in Islam. So I feel I have a fairly good knowledge of Islam. But at the same time, my parents have always pushed me to excel secularly, as well. That's why I'm doing medicine.

One of the things that my mom always taught me was the idea of holding fast to your religion and your identity, but at the same time, not letting that prevent you from making new friends and being exposed to different ideas. I have a wide base of friends—friends of different races, different backgrounds. I have a very progressive attitude. I know what ideals of my religion I need to maintain and uphold—things like having a working knowledge of the religion, praying five times a day, and fasting.

One thing that people who consider themselves religious in any religion fail to realize is how to apply the ideals and principles of the religion within a given space/time, within a modern-day perspective. For example, the Prophet rode a camel. But obviously, you're not going to be riding a camel in modern-day society. There are certain progressive changes that you have to adapt to—again, without sacrificing the inviolable and sacrosanct qualities, tenets, and practices of the religion.

And I think I was given an education that fostered that—what the Muslim community in America needs to do now, given this space/time we're in, in order to uphold the principles of the religion. And at the same time, you should be open to all the positive benefits that American society has to offer and, more importantly, all the positive benefits that we as Muslims have to offer American society to create a better America.

Crossroads

American Islam right now is sort of at a crossroads. On the one hand, there are the traditionalists who seek to go back to the way things were, with the idea that if the Prophet came down with his life as the paradigm, we should be following that paradigm to the fullest letter possible.

On the other hand, you have the more progressive side that advocates that there might be certain aspects of our tradition that we have to sacrifice in order to progress. Since we live in a certain country, we've got to dress a certain way, talk a certain way, and eat a certain way. The most obvious manifestation of this is that I'm a first-generation American and I don't speak like my parents at all. They have an accent. I don't.

I guess I'm sort of in the middle. I don't think that change is dangerous— I think it needs to be embraced. I don't think we have to sacrifice our beautiful history and tradition for the sake of survival. Yet I strongly believe that the survival of Islam and the Muslim community depends on how well we can relay those beautiful qualities in the language and modes of modern society. And I think that Muslims need to find a way to incorporate those positive aspects of their tradition and their history with the positive aspects of what American society has to offer and create this American Islam that, hopefully, will be a paradigm for everybody, whether they be Muslim or not.

I think the emerging American Islam will have the positive aspects of Arab Islam, of Indo-Pak Islam, and Malaysian and African Islam. Somehow we'll be able to amalgamate the positives and leave out some of the cultural baggage and negative aspects that all of these things have. That will be combined with an American mindset, an American language, an American way of dealing with people.

Knowledge

American society has a lot of positive things to offer. For example, Americans are the most generous people in the world. They did a study and found that, per capita, Americans give more wealth toward charitable causes than people anywhere else. That's an Islamic principle which Muslims really don't follow as much as they should. We harp on American bureaucracy for being inefficient, but it's the most efficient in the world. In the Middle East, you try to get even the simplest thing done—like a legal thing—it takes forever because there's no efficient bureaucracy. I think that's something that Muslims can learn.

There are other things, like knowledge—of science, philosophy, and psychology and sociology—those are things that Muslims need to understand, and I don't think we're doing that. I did an independent study course this semester analyzing why the Muslim empire crumbled, because for a long time they were the center of civilization. If we look at how Muslims ascended and reached that peak of human civilization, it was because they were interested in learning all available information. They studied the sciences and philosophy and every-thing that was there on the table.

And then they figured, "We've reached the pinnacle of success. We have the best religion out there. Nothing else needs to be changed and nothing else needs to be learned." Europe willingly learned from the Muslims, but it was an unthinkable thought for Muslims to learn from the so-called "infidels." And unfortunately, that was a mindset that dominated until 1700 and 1800, and by that time, the transmutation had elevated Europe to be the new pinnacle of civilization.

We've stopped learning, and we've stopped teaching. And that's sort of what's brought Muslims to the plight that they're in right now. This plight is the current political, economic, social, and religious debasement of the Muslim world compared to the amazing levels of accomplishment the Muslim civiliza-tion had demonstrated and imparted to the human condition. You can never reach a level where you say, "I don't need to know any more."

"Go to China."

I think we need to maintain a certain level of authenticity of what our tra-dition tells us and, at the same time, understand that we need to explore new horizons. Again, one of the things that the Prophet told us is to seek knowl-edge even if you have to "go to China." He never went to China, though. What people don't realize is that by saying this he indirectly says that whatever knowledge I've given you is not enough, that there's things you can learn from the Chinese. And just because they are unbelievers, don't think that you can't learn from them.

Unfortunately, there's a sort of mindset within the Muslim mentality right now that is, "We can't learn from those who are not Muslims because they're not following 'the true path of God.'" I think that's a really arrogant and pre-sumptuous mindset. And we need to shed that and understand that, yes, there are things that we can learn and hopefully incorporate, and there are things we can teach others, as well.

You can call me naive, but I really do have a positive outlook for the future of the American community at large. It's not just America versus the rest of the world. I think we are realizing that we are part of a global community. If one part of the community is ailing, it's everyone's responsibility to find out what's wrong and not just say, "It's not my problem."

We are realizing that we ourselves are the paradigm for the global community because American people are not one race—we're a conglomeration of different races. If anything, we're the ones who typify this concept of a global community, at least in theory. I have great hope.

It's One Small Step to Having Less Hate and Misunderstanding

Abra, 20
Jewish (Reform)

The last time I was at the Twin Towers was the July before September 11 happened. I went to a concert and took a ferry home. Before we took the ferry, we walked past them. I put my hand on one of the buildings, and I looked up, and I was like, "Wow . . . it's so tall, it's incredible." I haven't been back there since. It's like, if I don't go down there, maybe it's still the way that it was.

My mom works in a building next to the World Trade Center. There were two messages from my mom on our machine saying she had never made it across the Hudson River. She got to the Hoboken ferry—the first plane had already hit. They were standing there trying to get on the ferry when the second plane hit. That's when the attendant said, "This ferry isn't going anywhere. We're staying right here." My dad was evacuated from his Jersey City office and sent home.

Here I was—four days from starting college. This was supposed to be a big time for me, and the world was 180 degrees different. All the airports were closed. We had to drive almost all night to get to Chicago in time for registration. It was awful.

At first I thought it was a Palestinian terrorist organization because I had heard some newscasters throwing around rumors. But after, I found out it was Islamists. I don't think I knew very much about Islam at that point. I definitely know more and feel more comfortable about it now. Maybe the attack had something to do with it, because it forced the people in this country to learn more about Islam. Also, I'm an international-studies major studying the Middle East, so my academic interests span everything from interreligious dialogue to international-relations theory.

I deliberately put myself into a position to learn more about Islam. I deliberately make the choice to talk to Muslims. I feel that the small things I can do as an individual to be friends with Muslims—especially in light of the Middle East conflict—is at the heart of what I'm interested in.

Friends

I'm a Jewish-American and my friend is a Palestinian-American. In some ways, maybe in an emotional way—or even a physical way—we're safer around each other here than an Israeli and a Palestinian in the region itself. We can be friends here. If we can form that bond with each other, then we're lucky, because people in Israel and Palestine cannot do that. That's important for me—to make a deliberate effort to reach out to Muslims, because it's one small step to having less hate and misunderstanding.

I'm now involved in a Jewish-Muslim dialogue group. The first meeting was about getting to know each other. The one after that, we talked about the broad questions of "What is Judaism?" and "What is Islam?" The one after that, we discussed the basic tenets of Judaism and the basic tenets of Islam. The one after that was supposed to be on food. This one is on homosexuality. I want to do one on human rights—how each religion views human rights.

Throughout the month of November, it was Ramadan. So every day the Muslim Student Association was having an *iftar*, a break-the-fast, and they'd have food. I had an idea for an interfaith Ramadan break-the-fast, so I talked to my friends Will and Mohanned about it. Will's Christian, and Mohanned's Muslim. And so on November 25, we had the Jewish students and the students from Brent House—the Episcopalian center—come to Hillel and cook during the day. Then we served the food for the Muslim Student Association at Brent House, to try to get everybody in the same place just talking with each other. People loved it; they had a great time. The only faux pas was that I ended up sitting on the men's side of the room by accident! It's like a cultural habit that during the meal the Muslim guys will sit separately from the girls. In the spring we might do another event, like an interfaith mock Seder, for Passover.

No War Lasts Forever

I consider myself to be somewhat of a Zionist. Zionism is self-determination for Jews. It's pretty closely linked to the religion, but I don't think that all Jews feel that way. I want to move to Israel at some point in my life.

No war lasts forever. After there's peace between Jews and Arabs over there, there's going to be decades of reconciliation. I want to continue doing work in peace and conflict resolution and intergroup relations.

We've Got to Get Religion Involved in Bringing Folks Together

In June of 1998, when he was twenty-two years old, Eboo Patel had a vision of an organization that would unite young people of different faiths in service to their communities and the world. His organization became the Chicago-based Interfaith Youth Core, and Patel, who now has a doctorate in the sociology of religion, became a leader in the burgeoning interfaith youth movement. IFYC runs active youth programs in Chicago, organizes national conferences, and catalyzes new interfaith youth projects. Here Patel talks about the growth and significance of this movement.

Photo credit: Shehnaz Mansuri

Eboo Patel, 27
Muslim

In the 1960s, you had the best sociologists in the world saying religion is dead. Harvey Cox is the Harvard theologian who said famously that the rise of the metropolis and the demise of traditional religion are the two main hallmarks of our time and they are linked. It was in 1965, and his book was called *The Secular City*.

These guys were wrong, right? What you've seen in the past thirty years is the rise of political religiosity, largely on the conservative side. In America it's the religious right. In India it's the Hindu right. In the Muslim world it's the Muslim right. And in Israel it's the Jewish right. Not that they didn't exist beforehand, but they gained ascendancy and power in the last thirty years. And one of the main hallmarks of these conservative movements is "everybody else is wrong."

The other thing that happened was the end of the Cold War. And so this bipolar U.S.-Soviet world was in demise. What's the new world order? Some people say it's the clash of civilizations—it's Bosnian Muslim versus Serbian Orthodox, it's Israeli Jew versus Palestinian Muslim. That's how the world is going to be defined—by people battling over matters of identity. And the central matter of identity for the vast majority of the world is religious.

MY FAITH JOURNEY

And you have a bunch of people saying, "Hold on! Religion can't just be involved in people killing one another. We've got to get religion involved in bringing folks together." And that's why I think you get the emergence of the interfaith movement in the '90s.

September 11, I think, is the ultimate example of what we've seen over the last thirty or forty years of religion in the world. It is what I would call totalitarian religion—people who believe that their way is the only way and that everybody else should follow their way. It's that idea that is gaining high levels of power in our world.

The way that September 11 changed my work is that I don't have to convince people that religion counts anymore. Before September 11 people were like, "All right, you're bringing young people from different religions together. Sounds like a good thing. But it doesn't really matter on any kind of global scale. Why aren't you involved in antipoverty work? If you really want to make a difference, you'll do something about nation states being at war."

I'm saying, "You know what? There is no way that this world is going to get any better unless you get religious people involved." And after September 11 nobody argues with that. They might say, "What you need to do with religious people is make them less religious." But they know religious people have to be involved somehow.

Part of my job is to be respectful of people's religious identities. If you think that I'm going to hell, that's OK. But if you throw rocks at me, that's not OK. So the people who think I'm going to hell can still be nice to me—I don't think that's inconsistent at all. It's the people who think I'm going to hell and who don't want my mosque in their neighborhood—that's what I'm working against. **I'm not working to change people's theologies. I'm working to change the way we act on Earth for each other and for the Earth.**

Young people today have a visceral experience of diversity. They have friends from other backgrounds. But they are also people of faith and devotion. Part of the question is how what they're learning in the mosque or in the synagogue or in the church is relevant to the school or the baseball diamond or the playground or the movie theater. Is what you learn in the mosque only relevant to the mosque?

There are a lot of places where religious communities meet to talk about religion—synagogues and mosques and churches. And there are a lot of places where religiously diverse people meet—YMCAs, schools, and playgrounds. But there are very few places where religiously diverse people meet to talk about matters of religion. So what ends up happening is people are like, "OK, I'm in a diverse situation, but I don't talk about religion here." And then, "I'm in a religious situation, but I don't talk about diversity here."

If you leave that void of not talking about religion amongst religious diversity then something's going to fill that void—negative stereotypes will fill that void. If people don't talk about Muslims with Jews, Muslims, and Christians, then other people get ideas about what Muslims are about. So we're saying that we in America need to have a conversation about religious diversity. And that conversation should not be led by Pat Robertson. It should not be led by Franklin Graham. It should be led by well-meaning people in different faith communities talking about who they are.

"Shared values" is our approach. Our goal is to affirm the person's connection with their home tradition. It is to show them what they have in common with other traditions without diluting the uniqueness of each and to encourage them to work together to serve others. The methodology we use is called shared values.

For example, you bring people from different backgrounds together to talk about how their traditions speak to the value of hospitality. It retains the distinctiveness of each tradition because the kids speak from their own scripture, they speak from their own stories. The Good Samaritan story, the Exodus story, Sura 93—they speak to something in common. We get to it through different routes, but we all share hospitality. We can work on it together. We can clean a river together. We can do a CD together. We can build a house together. We can do a performance together. That's what we're suggesting. You need to build on that 'cause there are things that are not shared in religious communities. Do you ever get to those differences? We haven't figured that out yet. But we think that there's a ton of work to do on this other part.

What we are not about is planting the problems of religion in kids' minds. I think that there's enough of that done. I think it's totally fair to be critical of religious traditions. But we live in a world that is critical of those traditions. So part of our job is to highlight what is positive and important in those traditions. Just creating a space—that's not a house of worship—where people can say, "I'm religious" is powerful. It's a big deal.

MY FAITH JOURNEY

We don't deal a lot with beliefs. The central things on the table in an Interfaith Youth Core discussion are not "Is Jesus the Son of God as Christians believe? Or is he a prophet as Muslims believe?" What we talk about is what our religion means in the world. "How does Jesus inspire you to help others and to get along with people—whether he is the Son of God or a prophet?" And part of the reason we do that is because we want to respect the private space of religious individuals, their families, and their communities. And part of the reason is because it's just not a fruitful discussion.

There are a lot of young people from different religious backgrounds in interaction. And the big question is—how are they going to interact? Are they going to kill each other? Are they going to say, "We need to work together on our shared values of protecting life, of loving the Earth, of building free and open societies?"

So what we are doing is saying, "We want to create spaces where young people from religiously diverse backgrounds can come together to deal with matters of religious diversity in a manner which builds understanding and serves others, serves the broader society." It's becoming a movement. We at this organization are intent on building that movement.

This city, Chicago, is where the first formal interfaith event happened—the World's Parliament of Religions in 1893. There are number of groups that have emerged to live up to that history—the National Conference for Community and Justice, the Council for a Parliament of the World's Religions. The Interfaith Service House was here for a couple of years. This organization [IFYC] emerged in 1998. And in the last ten years, a number of interfaith organizations have started.

One of our interns started a group at the University of Illinois called Bridges. It brings together Jews and Arabs, basically. Then there's Jewish-Muslim dialogue groups at the University of Chicago, New York University, Yale. There's a Multifaith Council, which was established by a guy named Victor Kazanjian. He has worked with colleges and universities across the country on matters of religious diversity.

Just last month, we brought thirty of these people together for what we think is the first national conference that's trying to build the interfaith youth movement. The first thing that we have to do is talk about what we're doing. How are you doing this work in the South Bronx? How are you doing it in

Houston? What's your model? And then, how can we network our initiatives and take some collective next steps forward?

Amongst other things, we are going to publish a book on interfaith youth work. How are different people doing this work? And then we're putting together a national day of interfaith youth service in fifteen cities across the country. You'll have thousands of kids from different faith communities coming together to do a service project and sharing how their diverse religious traditions inspire social-justice work.

I would say that the fountainhead of a lot of this stuff is Harvard's Pluralism Project, which we've worked closely with, also. They have turned young people into knowledge producers. What Diana Eck has done is to say, "In my world-religions classrooms I have Muslims, Hindus, Jews. If we want to know about religious pluralism in America, send them back to their home communities armed with research tools, tape recorders, and questions."

So you have these nineteen-year-old kids going back to Santa Fe, Austin, Kansas City, and St. Louis asking: "Mom, Dad, how did we build a Hindu temple?" "How did we build a mosque?" "What problems did we have with the zoning board?" "How did you raise the money?"

So that has served as a model for us here. Our young people don't have to just go through a program. They can produce media. They can be contributing a voice to the world. This is a whole different way of thinking about young people. We don't just think about young people in how they learn, but also in what they can teach because of the intuitive sense of diversity that they have.

Please see www.ifyc.org for more information about the Interfaith Youth Core.

Resources

This book raises more questions than it answers. I hope readers will be inspired to learn more about their own faiths and the faiths of others and to explore the issues discussed in these pages. This new chapter presents a short resource list—books and organizations— that can be helpful. These are just a few of the many fine resources available in libraries, bookstores, and on the Internet.

General Books

Armstrong, Karen. *A History of God: The 4,000-Year Quest of Judaism, Christianity and Islam* (New York: Random House, 1994).
> Explores how the concept of God evolved in the world's three major monotheistic religions.
The Battle for God (New York: Random House, 2000).
> Examines the growth of religious fundamentalism around the world, especially Protestant fundamentalism in the United States, Jewish fundamentalism in Israel, and Islamic fundamentalism in Iran and Egypt.

Eck, Diana L. *A New Religious America: How a "Christian Country" Has Become the World's Most Religiously Diverse Nation* (San Francisco: Harper, 2001).
> Describes how a variety of religious traditions are flourishing in the United States today.

Esposito, John L., Darrell J. Fasching, and Todd Lewis. *World Religions Today* (New York: Oxford Univ. Press, 2001).
> A survey of the world's major religious traditions, including their histories, development, and status in today's world.

Feiler, Bruce. *Abraham: A Journey to the Heart of Three Faiths* (New York: William Morrow, 2002).
> A look at the life and legacy of Abraham, the shared "father" of the Jewish, Muslim, and Christian faiths.

Fowler, James W. *Stages of Faith: The Psychology of Human Development* (San Francisco: Harper, 1995).
> A luminary in the field of psychology of religion, Fowler spoke to hundreds of people of disparate religious backgrounds (as well as the nonreligious) to explore the developmental stages of faith and how people find meaning and purpose in their lives.

Gellman, Marc, and Thomas Hartman. *How Do You Spell God? Answers to the Big Questions from Around the World* (New York: Beech Tree, 1995).
> Written for children ages 10 and up, this book examines how different religions approach and respond to important spiritual questions.

Matlins, Stuart M., and Arthur J. Magida, eds. *How to Be a Perfect Stranger: The Essential Religious Etiquette Handbook* (Woodstock, Vt: Skylight Paths, 2003).
> A guidebook to the practices, customs, and ceremonies of a wide variety of faiths.

Smith, Huston. *The World's Religions* (San Francisco: Harper, 1991).
> Presents the essential aspects and teachings of the world's major religions.
Forgotten Truth: The Common Vision of the World's Religions (San Francisco: Harper, 1992).
> An examination of the characteristics shared by the great religious traditions.

Sweeney, John M., and the editors at Skylight Paths. *God Within: Our Spiritual Future—As Told by Today's New Adults* (Solon, Ohio: CoNexus Press).
> Through writing and art, young Americans describe what it means to be young and spiritual today.

Christianity

Brown, Raymond E. *An Introduction to the New Testament* (New York: Doubleday, 1997).
An analysis of the books of the New Testament with commentary by a respected scholar.

Chidester, David. *Christianity: A Global History* (San Francisco: Harper, 2000).
Summarizes 2,000 years of Christian history.

Lewis, C. S. *Mere Christianity* (San Francisco: Harper, 2001).
An enduring book originally published in 1952 about the Christian faith by one of the greatest writers of the twentieth century.

Pagels, Elaine. *Beyond Belief: The Secret Gospel of Thomas* (New York: Random House, 2003).
Explores how diversity in early Christian thought was suppressed and how the texts and beliefs that define Christianity today became dominant.

Smith, Christian. *Christian America? What Evangelicals Really Want* (Berkeley: Univ. of California Press, 2002).
Using statistical research and in-depth interviews with 200 Protestant evangelicals across the United States, Smith reveals the enormous diversity in their views, beliefs, and values.

Interfaith Families

Kovacs, Patty. *A Time to Heal: An Overview of the Histories of Judaism and Catholicism: 396–2002 CE* (Chicago: Interfaith Religious Education Books).
Provides special tools for children of interfaith marriages, emphasizing the healing that families can do to bridge the historical divisions that have existed for centuries between Judaism and Christianity.
The God We Share (Chicago: Interfaith Religious Education Books).
An overview of the development and curriculum of the Chicago Family School for interfaith (Jewish-Christian) families.
For ordering information, e-mail kovacs@ameritech.net. Other titles are available.

Islam

Ali, Abdullah Yusuf. *The Meaning of the Holy Qur'an* (Beltsville: Amana Pubns., 2001).
A well-known translation of the Qur'an from Arabic to English.

Armstrong, Karen. *Muhammad: A Biography of the Prophet* (San Francisco: Harper, 1993).
An account of the life, works, and teachings of the Prophet Muhammad.

Diouf, Sylviane. *Servants of Allah: African Muslims Enslaved in the Americas* (New York: New York Univ. Press, 1998).
Describes the journey of slaves, many of whom were Muslims, from West Africa to the Americas, and analyzes the impact of Islam on African-Americans and American society.

Esposito, John L. *What Everyone Needs to Know about Islam* (New York: Oxford Univ. Press, 2002).
Addresses the questions many non-Muslims have about Islam.

Hasan, Asma Gull. *American Muslims: The New Generation* (New York: Continuum, 2001).
Written by a young American-born Muslim woman, the book debunks stereotypes about Muslims and describes the evolution of Islam in the United States.

Judaism

Cahill, Thomas. *The Gifts of the Jews: How a Tribe of Desert Nomads Changed the Way Everyone Thinks and Feels* (New York: Anchor, 1999).
A linear theory of history is just one of the Jewish contributions to western civilization that is discussed in this book.

Hyman, Meryl. *Who is a Jew? Conversations, Not Conclusions* (Woodstock, Vt: Jewish Lights Pub., 1999).
A collection of conversations with 35 religious leaders about what defines a Jew.

Jewish Publication Society. *Tanakh: The Holy Scriptures, The New JPS Translation According to the Traditional Hebrew Text* (Philadelphia: Jewish Publication Society, 1988).
Developed over 30 years by rabbis and scholars, this contemporary English translation includes the Torah, Nevi'im (The Prophets), and Kethuvim (The Writings).

Plaskow, Judith. *Standing Again at Sinai: Judaism from a Feminist Perspective* (San Francisco: Harper, 1991).
A feminist critique of Judaism and an analysis of how Jewish tradition can be shaped by the inclusion of women's voices and experiences.

Seltzer, Robert M. *Jewish People, Jewish Thought* (Upper Saddle River, NJ: Prentice Hall, 2003).
A comprehensive primer on Jewish history and thought.

Memoirs and Biographies

Dubner, Stephen J. *Turbulent Souls: A Catholic Son's Return to His Jewish Family* (New York: William Morrow, 1999).
The son of Jews who converted to Catholicism, the author describes his journey back to Judaism.

Lewis, C.S. *Surprised by Joy: The Shape of My Early Life* (Harvest Books, 1966).
One of the greatest Christian scholars describes his conversion from atheism to Christianity.

Malcolm X, et al. *The Autobiography of Malcolm X* (African American Images, 1989).
A powerful memoir about transformation—the transformation of a man from a petty thief to a civil rights leader—and the role that Islam played in his life.

White, Mel. *Stranger at the Gate: To Be Gay and Christian in America* (New York: Plume, 1995).
An evangelical minister who was a speechwriter for Christian right leaders reconciles his faith with his homosexuality after enduring 25 years of self-loathing.

Winner, Lauren F. *Girl Meets God: On the Path to a Spiritual Life* (Chapel Hill: Algonquin Books, 2002).
Chronicles the young author's intense search for spiritual meaning and identity that leads her from Orthodox Judaism to Christianity.

Organizations

URLs frequently change; if a Web site address listed below has become invalid, you may need to plug the name of the organization into a search engine.

Christian
Christian Coalition of America
www.cc.org
> An organization founded by conservative Christian evangelist Pat Robertson to give Christians a voice in government.

Greek Orthodox Archdiocese of America
www.goarch.org
> Provides leadership to Greek Orthodox churches ministering to 1.5 million followers in the United States.

National Council of Churches
www.ncccusa.org
> An ecumenical community of 36 Protestant, Anglican, and Orthodox member denominations.

Vatican: The Holy See
www.vatican.va
> The Web site of the governing body of Roman Catholicism in Rome, Italy.

World Council of Churches
www.wcc-coe.org
> Brings together churches, fellowships, and denominations representing about 400 million Christians around the world.

Jewish
Anti-Defamation League
www.adl.org
> Monitors and combats anti-Semitism and other forms of bigotry.

B'nai B'rith Youth Organization
www.bbyo.org
> Provides opportunities for Jewish teenagers to develop leadership skills, self-esteem, appreciation of Jewish religion and culture, and friendships with other Jewish youth.

National Conference of Synagogue Youth
www.ou.org/NCSY
> An organization affiliated with the Orthodox movement that is open to all Jewish youth.

North American Federation of Temple Youth
http://nfty.org
> An organization for high-school-aged Jewish youth of the Reform movement.

United Synagogue Youth
www.usy.org
> An organization for Jewish teenagers of the Conservative movement.

Muslim

American Society of Muslims
National Young Adult Association
www.masyoungadult.org/study/links.html
> The youth group affiliated with the American Society of Muslims—an organization of American Muslims, mostly African-Americans, founded by Elijah Muhammed, former Nation of Islam leader.

Council on American-Islamic Relations
www.cair-net.org
> Educates non-Muslims about Islam. Challenges negative stereotypes and promotes a positive image of Islam and Muslims.

Islamic Society of North America
www.isna.net
> Works for the betterment of the Muslim community and society.

Young Muslims
www.ymsite.com
> Educates, trains, and develops Muslim youth.

Interfaith

Council for a Parliament of the World's Religions
www.cpwr.org
> Promotes harmony between religious and spiritual communities and brings them together to achieve a better world.

Interfaith Youth Core (IFYC)
www.ifyc.org
> Brings young people from different faith communities together to deepen their own religious identities, build bridges between faith communities, and work collectively to serve others. IFYC's "Sacred Stories Project" is a CD of voices of Muslim, Jewish, and Christian youth reflecting on the ethic of hospitality and how religious figures—Abraham, Jesus, the Muslim Caliph Umar—inspire acts of hospitality today.

The Pluralism Project
www.pluralism.org
> Studies the increasing religious diversity of the United States and works to increase religious tolerance.

The United Religions Initiative
www.uri.org
> Brings together from around the globe people of different faith backgrounds with the goal of creating a just, peaceful world.

Campus

Catholic Campus Ministry Association
www.ccmanet.org

Chi Alpha Campus Ministries, USA (Christian)
www.chialpha.com

Hillel: The Foundation for Jewish Campus Life
www.hillel.org

InterVarsity Christian Fellowship/USA (Evangelical Christian)
www.intervarsity.org

Muslim Students Association of the US & Canada
www.msa-national.org

National Catholic Student Coalition
www.catholicstudent.org

Orthodox Christian Fellowship
www.ocf.net

Church and State Separation

American Atheists
www.atheists.org
Lobbies for the civil liberties of atheists and the separation of government and religion.

American Civil Liberties Union
www.aclu.org
Defends Americans' civil liberties, including the freedom to practice or not practice religion.

Americans United for Separation of Church and State
www.au.org
Defends religious diversity and fights threats to church-state separation.